NOAH'S ARK

Michael Harrison and Christopher Stuart-Clark

OXFORD UNIVERSITY PRESS 1983

Oxford University Press, Walton Street, Oxford OX2 6DP
Oxford London Glasgow
New York Toronto Melbourne Auckland
Kuala Lumpur Singapore Hong Kong Tokyo
Delhi Bombay Calcutta Madras Karachi
Nairobi Dar es Salaam Cape Town

and associated companies in
Beirut Berlin Ibadan Mexico City Nicosia

Oxford is a trade mark of Oxford University Press

This selection © Michael Harrison and Christopher Stuart-Clark 1983

British Library Cataloguing in Publication Data
Harrison, Michael
 Noah's ark.
 1. Bible. O.T. Genesis—Juvenile literature
 2. Noah's ark—Juvenile literature
 I. Title   II. Stuart-Clark, Christopher
 222'.11   BS580.N6
 ISBN 0–19–276047–5

Typeset by Wyvern Typesetting Ltd, Bristol
Printed in Hong Kong

Contents

Stories of the Flood   5

**Every living creature
an A–Z of beasts and birds**   35

God loosed the rain   88

Then died the corrupted beasts   95

Noah sends the raven and the dove   101

The animals leave the ark   112

Go forth and multiply   119

A second flood   127

Postscript   137

Acknowledgements   138

Index of titles and first lines   140

Stories of the Flood

The story of the Great Flood and how all the animals we know today were saved, along with one man's family, has been told in many different ways all over the world.

One of the earliest versions is from Babylon, in a story known as the Epic of Gilgamesh:

The Gilgamesh Flood

After the gods had made man, there came a time when there were just too many people making too much noise. They made so much that even the storm god Enlil could not sleep. He called a meeting of the gods and said to them, 'This racket keeps me awake. Men are bellowing like wild oxen. Let us destroy them, every one of them. Let the wind blow, and let the storm rage. Let *them* suffer some noise in their turn. Yes, let the storm rage until flood overwhelms the land and swallows them up.'

When they heard these terrible words the other gods cried out in horror, but Enlil would not listen. Ea, the wise god of water, decided secretly to save his favourite, the King, from this flood so that there would still be men left to serve the gods with the sacrifices they loved.

That night he filled the King's dreams with howling hurricanes and waves crashing over his house. The King woke sweating in such terror that he rushed to the temple and called out, 'Ea! Ea! What does this nightmare mean?'

Ea answered his favourite, 'I cannot tell any man the secrets of the gods. You must go home. When you get there, lean your head against the wall of your house.'

So the King went slowly back to his house and leaned his head against the wall, the wall made of reeds. After a while he heard a voice saying, 'You! Reed-house! Wake up and listen! Enlil is going to flood the world to silence all the people. The King would be able to save his life if he knew this because he could build a boat and take into it the seed of every living thing.' The King sat with his head against the reed wall while Ea went on pretending to talk to the house, giving exact instructions for the boat.

In the morning the King called his craftsmen together and ordered them to collect huge piles of rope and timber and barrels of pitch. He made them build a ship of seven storeys, the top one as large as an acre of land. When all was finished he sent inside his family, his relations and his craftsmen, and after them the birds and beasts. That evening the rain began to fall gently.

At the end of that night there was no dawn. It stayed dark, as dark as death, except when the dreadful lightning flashed out. The rain fell so hard that you wouldn't have been able to tell which was sea and which was sky. The noise . . . the noise drove men mad as it crashed into their skulls. Even the gods were terrified by what Enlil's rage had let loose. For six days and nights the storm continued but on the seventh day the rain stopped, the waters grew quiet, and a great calm fell. As the King opened a window, light streamed in and the warm rays of the sun lit up the dark corners of the boat. The King looked out over the still and silent sea. Although the rain had stopped, tears ran down his face as he wept for his people.

The boat floated quietly all that day, and next morning it grounded on a mountain top and there it stayed for six days. On the seventh day the King let out a dove, but she returned as she could not find any other place to rest. He released a swallow next but she too returned. Finally a raven was sent out. When she saw that the water had gone down, she flew round cawing before flying off. And so the King released all the birds in one great coloured cloud and built a fire of cedar wood to sacrifice to the gods.

When Enlil smelt the offering he was furious at first but then Ea said to him, 'Why must you try to destroy mankind? When they grow wild, rein them in, don't rain them out altogether. Instead of a flood, why not send a ravening lion? Instead of a flood, why not a drought? Instead of a flood, why not disease? Punish, weed out, but do not wipe out our handiwork.'

Enlil was moved by Ea's words and grew sorry for what he had done. He took the King and his wife and said to them, 'Because you were wise enough to learn from a dream what I had planned, you, of all mankind, shall enjoy everlasting life and shall walk for ever in the garden of the gods at the place of the sunrise.'

Michael Richards

Some Indians on the North-West Pacific coast of America had a different version of the same story:

Mount Rainier and the Great Flood

Long, long ago, when the earth was young, the Great Spirit became very angry with the people and the animals of his world. The Great Spirit lived on the snowy summit of Takhoma.

He was angry because the people and animals were wicked and did many mean things to each other. He decided that he would rid the earth of all of them except the good animals and one good man and his family.

So he said to the good man, 'Shoot an arrow into that cloud hanging low over the mountain.'

The good man shot an arrow, and it stuck in the cloud.

'Now shoot another arrow into the shaft of that arrow,' continued the Great Spirit.

The second arrow hit the lower part of the first arrow and stuck there. The man kept on shooting arrows, as the Great Spirit commanded, and each arrow stuck in the lower part of the preceding arrow. After a while there was a long rope of arrows reaching from the cloud on top of the mountain clear down to the ground.

'Now tell your wife and children,' commanded the Great Spirit, 'to climb up that rope of arrows. Tell the good animals to climb up after them. But don't let the bad people and the bad animals go up.'

So the good man sent his wife up the arrow rope, then his children, and then the good animals. He watched them climb into the cloud above the mountain. Then the good man himself climbed up.

Just as he was stepping into the cloud, he looked back. Coming up the arrow rope was a long line of bad animals and snakes. They were climbing toward the cloud. So the good man took hold of the arrow nearest him and broke the rope. He watched all the bad animals and the snakes tumble down the sides of the mountain.

When the Great Spirit saw that the good animals and the good people were safe around him, he caused a heavy rain to fall. It rained and rained and rained for many days and many nights. All the earth was under water. The water rose higher and higher on the sides of Takhoma. At last it came up to the snow line, up to the high place where the snow leaves off in the summertime.

By that time all the bad people and all the bad animals were drowned. So the Great Spirit commanded the rain to stop. He and the good man and his family watched the waters slowly go down. The land became dry again.

Then the Great Spirit said to the good man, 'Now you may take your family and the animals back to the earth.'

So they all climbed out of the cloud, and the good man led them down a mountain-trail to the place where they were to build a new lodge. As they walked down, they found no bad animals or snakes, and there have been none on Takhoma to this day.

Ella Clark

The Squamish Indians who lived in British Columbia told this story:

Mount Baker and the Great Flood

When the Squamish people saw the great flood coming, they gathered on a spot above the reach of the water. There they held a big council. To save their tribe from destruction, they decided to build a giant canoe and tie it to a giant rock. Day and night the men worked, building a boat larger than any of them had ever seen. The women made the rope for fastening it to the rock. They gathered cedar fibre, tore it into shreds, rolled it and chewed it and worked it into a larger rope than any of them had ever seen. Then they oiled it.

The people fastened one end of the giant rope to the giant canoe, and the other end to a huge rock. Then they put into the canoe every baby and every small child. They placed enough food and fresh water in the boat to last for many days.

Then they chose two guardians for the children—the mother of the youngest baby in the camp, and the bravest and best of their young men. They placed him in the stern of the canoe and seated the young mother, a girl of sixteen, with her baby, only two weeks old, in the bow. No one else tried to get into the boat. No one wailed or wept as the water reached the hilltop where they had gathered. No one wept as the canoe floated away. The people left behind sank beneath the flood.

For days the children and their young guardians saw only a world of water and sky. But the rope held. One morning they saw, far to the south, a speck on top of the water. When the sun reached the middle of the sky, the speck was a big spot. By the time the sun reached the water, the spot was still larger.

When the moon came up, the man thought he saw a piece of land. All night he watched it. In the morning, when the sun came out of the water, the young man saw a mountain—Mount Baker it is called now. He cut the rope and paddled toward the south. By the time the canoe reached the mountain, the upper half of the peak was dry.

On the mountain the guardians helped the children out of the boat. When the waters had gone down and the land below was dry, they made a new camp. They built their lodges between the Fraser River and the Georgia Strait, in sight of Mount Baker. The children lived and grew up. Through them the Squamish people were saved.

In a giant crack halfway up the slope of Mount Baker is the outline of the giant canoe. It has been there ever since the great flood.

Ella Clark

The story of Noj and the Flood comes from the Russian people of Siberia:

Noj and the Flood

Noj was a good man at a time when every other man was bad; or so God thought. At any rate he had decided to drown the lot of them, all except Noj, whom he warned in a whisper, 'Build a boat, Noj, build a boat.' And since Noj was accustomed to obeying the word of God, so he did, going deep into the forest each day and building it secretly from the best timbers. The only other person who knew about it was his wife.

The Devil grew very curious. He sidled up to Noj's wife one morning and said, 'Do me a favour, lady, tell me just what that man of yours is up to.'

'Certainly not,' said Noj's wife virtuously. 'It's between him and me and God, and has nothing whatever to do with you.'

'Suppose,' said the Devil, 'I were to offer you . . .'

'And whatever can you offer me, you ugly little runt?'

'A sweet tongue,' said the Devil, 'for a start; or beauty, or anything you like, a lighter hand with the baking, a speedier hand on the spindle; if only you tell me what Noj is making in the forest.'

'If I did,' said Noj's wife, 'I can't see you providing them.'

'Well then, wouldn't you like to know why Noj is doing whatever he is doing in the forest? Did he tell you that? Don't say you haven't been a little anxious.'

'I did wonder, that is the truth,' said Noj's wife, 'I hope he's not crazy, but . . .'

'So what harm can there be in it?'

Noj's wife sighed. 'Would you promise to tell me anything you find out?'

'Cross my heart, lady, and hope to die,' the Devil said.

So Noj's wife told the Devil that Noj was building a boat. And the Devil looked wise and went away and when he came back a few hours later told her that God was planning to send them on a long sea voyage, but he couldn't tell her why because even Noj didn't know that yet.

'But how's he going to get the boat from the forest to the river?' asked Noj's wife in astonishment.

'Perhaps he could do with some advice from me,' said the Devil and went away again. But from that time on, while Noj continued to build his boat by day, at night, secretly, the Devil crept in and undid his work, pulling out nails and breaking up timbers; thus each morning Noj had to begin work all over again.

'There's a jinx on me,' said Noj, crossly. 'At this rate I'll never get it done before the flood comes.' He worked harder and harder but all to no avail, and every day the skies grew heavier. Noj prayed to God then, but God was too busy preparing for the flood to take any notice of the Devil's activities (indeed he did not think he needed to, now that he planned to wipe out all the Devil's disciples). Nor did he hear Noj's prayer; until one day, at last, great drops of rain began to fall. Noj laid down his hammer and his saw and got down on his knees and prayed to God harder than ever.

'It's much too soon, God, my boat is not nearly finished, through no fault of mine. In fact I was beginning to think you didn't want me to finish it. Yet you promised to save us. Oh help me, God.' At that moment Noj's wife appeared with all her children clinging to her skirts and all her chickens and cows and pigs and sheep behind.

'I thought your boat could save us, husband, but whatever kind of boat is this?' she said. For the boat had only ribs and framework still, it had no planking, let alone a cabin with a roof, made of stout timbers caulked with pitch as Noj had planned it. 'Oh woe, oh woe, we'll all be drowned,' cried she.

From beyond the forest her cries were echoed as the waters rose; men climbed to the tops of their houses and clung to them helplessly, lashed by rain and wind. They took their animals with them if they could, all the rest were left floating on the tide. Noj and his family dragged themselves and their animals up the framework of his boat until they reached the highest point. But the waters went on rising all the time. And now dead people came floating past besides dead animals.

'Oh God,' prayed Noj, 'I am a virtuous man and why did you tell me to build my boat if you did not want me saved?'

'Oh God,' prayed Noj's wife, 'why did you ever let me have anything to do with the Devil?'

The water was already about their feet. But now something else moved gently towards them—'Like a *boat*,' cried one of the children. 'It *is* a boat,' another said. It struck the timbers of Noj's unfinished boat with a dull clang and waited while they all scrambled down to it. But they did not find wood beneath their feet this time. When they bent down and touched the deck, their hands met something cool and smooth and hard, that glimmered faintly in the dying light, that was the same colour as the rain itself. 'This boat is made of iron,' said Noj. 'God has sent it to us surely. There never was such a miracle.'

'Better than a lighter hand with the baking or speedier hand with the spindle any day,' said his wife. But Noj did not know what she was talking about.

So it was that Noj and his wife and their children, their chickens and cows and pigs and sheep were saved from the flood that engulfed all the rest of mankind. They floated away on their iron boat while the thunder boomed and the lightning flashed and the rain fell unceasingly. In the end there was no land to be seen at all.

And if when the flood subsided they were the only people left upon earth, nonetheless there they were and it wasn't wholly the Devil's to do what he liked with. One thing was certain, Noj's wife would never listen to that voice again: though one can't say the same of all her descendants.

Penelope Farmer

But the best-known story of the Great Flood is that of Noah and his family and the building of the Ark for the animals:

Noah's Flood

For a while God stayed his hand, but there came a generation when He saw that unless He cleansed the world of its sickness there would be no life left that was not diseased beyond cure. Still in His mercy He waited. At last there was just one man in all the world who remembered the true worship of God, and kept faith with man, and guarded his children against corruption. Noah was his name.

In a dream that was not a dream God spoke to Noah and showed him a ship, riding on stormy waters. It had neither mast nor sail nor rudder, but a full two hundred paces was its length, and thirty paces its breadth, and it was taller than the tallest cedar. One great door opened in its side, and a little window in its roof, and it was all black with tar.

'This you must build,' said God.

Noah woke, and prayed and gave thanks. Then he sent for his sons and they pulled down all his barns, saving the timber. He took money, all that he had, and bought more timber, and pitch, and canvas. He hired carpenters and paced out the ground and told them what they must build. So Noah made the boat God had showed him, a wonder of the world; standing black on the bare fields where his crops had grown.

Now God spoke in the hearts of all the animals of the world, according to their capacities. Two of every kind He chose, male and female, perfect, without scar or sore, and they gathered towards the

fields of Noah, creeping, flying, running, or burrowing through the earth. In the day and hour when the last peg was driven home they marched, orderly as a king's army, up the ramp and through the great door in the side of the boat. And God restored to them the condition of Eden so that the beasts of prey could eat the fodder which the sons of Noah had stored in the boat.

In the day and hour when the last animal passed the door, and Noah and his family drew up the ramp to close it, God loosed the rain. And more than rain. He loosed the under seas upon the land. For you must know that above the sky are waters and below the earth are waters, and only the strong hand of God holds them apart so that His world may live between. For His cleansing of that world He loosed His hold and the blue waters of the sky came streaming down and the black waters of the abyss came roaring up and the world was drowned. Then died the giants and the heroes and the women skilled in sorcery. Then died the corrupted men—and the corrupted beasts also, the winged lions and the sphinxes, the dragons and the unicorns, and none was ever seen again.

Only the boat which Noah had built floated on the water, a huge black coffin containing all the life that lived. In that darkness Noah prayed and gave thanks, and all the creatures with him prayed and gave thanks also, according to their capacities.

For forty full days and forty full nights—and the nights were no blacker than the days—they listened to the boom of rain upon the roof and the roar and suck of waves against the hull. But at last the noises ceased, as God stilled the storm and commanded the waters to withdraw to their ancient places. For another twenty days Noah waited, and then he opened the little window which God had shown

him he must make in the roof and cast one of the ravens up into the sky. The bird rose, croaking with the shock of light. Noah watched it circle, fly east, fly west, and settle back to his hand, so he knew that there was no land yet to be seen.

Seven days later he took one of the pigeons and cast it up, watching it spiral into the blue of noon, but then like the raven it circled back down to his hand.

Seven days later still, he took the other pigeon and cast it up. It rose circling as before, and then with a slap of wings sped eastwards, out of sight. He waited at the window until the sun was low, and there, gliding out of the dusk, was his pigeon. When it settled onto his hand he saw that it had gathered material for a nest, a twig of fresh olive with the leaf-buds just breaking into silver, so he knew that somewhere the land was dry.

Seven days later still he cast the same pigeon out and this time it did not return.

Next morning Noah and his sons let down the ramp and gazed from the sill of the door to see where the storm had blown them. The keel had come to rest on the great mountain Ararat in the far north. Far down in all the valleys gleamed the still-receding waters, half-veiled by mist where the slopes of the mountain steamed under God's strong sun, but at their feet the grass-blades were succulent with quick growth.

God spoke His word again in the hearts of all the animals so that they came marching out, orderly as a king's army, and began to scatter along the range seeking new lairs and new pastures. A soft wind blew the last of the storm-clouds westward and as Noah gazed he saw a shining arch of many colours building itself against the blackness of the cloud.

Once more God spoke in Noah's heart.

'This is My sign, My promise. Never again will I loose the waters to cleanse the world, but from this day on season will follow season and harvest harvest, all in their true order.'

So Noah gazed at the shining arch, and the cleanness of the world which God had given back to him, and he and all his family prayed and gave thanks.

Peter Dickinson

In the Middle Ages the story was told in England in the form of a play called a 'Miracle Play':

GOD   I, God, that all the world have wrought,
Heaven and Earth, and all of nought,
I see my people in deed and thought
Are foully set in sin.

Man that I made I will destroy,
Beast, worm and fowl to fly,
For on earth they me annoy
The folk that are therein.

Therefore, Noah, my servant free,
That righteous man art, as I see,
A ship soon thou shalt make thee
Of trees dry and light.

Destroyed all the world shall be,
Save thou, thy wife, thy sons three,
And their wives also with thee
Shall saved be, for thy sake.

NOAH   Ah, Lord, I thank thee loud and still
That to me art in such will
And spares me and my house to spill
As now I soothly find.

Have done, you men and women all!
Help, for aught that may befall,
To build this ship, chamber and hall,
As God hath bidden us do.

SHEM   Father, I am all ready bound.
An axe I have here, by my crown,
As sharp as any in all this town
For to go thereto.

HAM   I have a hatchet wonder keen,
To bite well, as may be seen.
A better ground one, as I ween
Is not in all this town.

JAPHET   And I can well make a pin
           And with this hammer knock it in.
           Go and work without more din,
           And I am ready bound.

NOAH'S WIFE   And we shall bring timber, too,
           For we can nothing else do.
           Women be weak to undergo
           Any great travail.

SHEM'S WIFE   Here is a good hacking-stock
           On this you may hew and knock.
           Shall none be idle in this flock,
           Nor now may no man fail.

HAM'S WIFE   And I will go to gather pitch
           The ship for to caulk and pitch.
           Anointed it must be, every stitch,
           Board, tree and pin.

JAPHET'S WIFE   And I will gather chips here
           To make a fire for you in cheer
           And for to dight your dinner
           Against you come in.

           (*Noah starts to build*)

NOAH   Now in the name of God I will begin
           To make the ship that we shall in,
           That we be ready for to swim
           At the coming of the flood.

           These boards here I join together
           To keep us safe from the weather,
           That we may row both hither and thither
           And safe be from this flood.

           Of this tree will I make the mast
           Tied with cables that will last,
           With a sail-yard for each blast,
           And each thing in their kind.

With top-castle and bowsprit,
With cords and ropes I have all fit
To sail forth at the next wet.
This ship is at an end.

Wife, in this castle we shall be kept.
My children and thou, I would in leapt.

NOAH'S WIFE   In faith, Noah, I had as lief thou slept
For all thy frankish fare.
I will not do after thy rede.

NOAH   Good wife, do now as I thee bid.

NOAH'S WIFE   In faith, not ere I see more need,
Though thou stand all the day and stare.

NOAH   Lord, that women be crabbed aye,
And never are meek, that dare I say.
This is well seen by me today
In witness of you each one.

Good wife, let be all this cheer
That thou makest in this place here;
For all they ween thou art master,—
And so thou art, I own.

GOD   Noah, take thou thy company
And in the ship hie that you be,
For none so righteous man to me
Is now on earth living.

Of beasts and fowls with thee thou take
Two and two, mate to mate,
He and she, ere thou slack
Against I send the weather.

NOAH   Have done, you men and women all!
Hie you, lest this water fall,
That each beast were in his stall
And into the ship brought.

21

(The animals go in)

SHEM Sir, here are lions, leopards in,
Horses, mares, oxen and swine,
Goats, calves, sheep and kine
Here sitting thou may see.

HAM Camels, asses, men may find,
Buck, doe, hart and hind,
And beasts of all manner kind
Here be, as thinketh me.

JAPHET Take here cats and dogs too,
Otter, fox, marten also,
Hares hopping gaily can go,
Have kale here for to eat.

NOAH'S WIFE And here are bears, wolves set,
Apes, owls, marmoset,
Weasels, squirrels and ferret,
Here they eat their meat.

SHEM'S WIFE Yet more beasts are in this house,
Here cats in a drowse,
Here a rat and here a mouse,
They stand nigh together.

HAM'S WIFE And here are fowls less and more,
Herons, cranes and bittern,
Swans, peacocks—and them before
Food for this weather.

JAPHET'S WIFE Here are cocks, kites, crows,
Rooks, raven, many rows,
Cuckoos, curlews. Whoever knows
Each one in his kind?

And here are doves, ducks, drakes,
Redshanks running through the lakes,
And each fowl that singing makes
In this ship men may find.

NOAH	Wife, come in. Why standest thou there? Thou art ever froward, that dare I swear. Come in, in God's name, time it were, For fear lest that we drown.
NOAH'S WIFE	I will not do after thy rede.
NOAH	Good wife, do now as I thee bid.
NOAH'S WIFE	In faith, not ere I see more need Though thou stand all the day and stare.
NOAH	Lord, that women be crabbed ay, And never are meek, that dare I say. That is well seen by me today In witness of you each one.
NOAH'S WIFE	Yea, sir, set up your sail And row forth with evil hale, For, without any fail, I will not out of this town. Unless I have my gossips every one One foot further I will not go. They shall not drown, by Saint John, If I may save their life. They loved me full well, I wist. Unless thou wilt let them in thy chest, Else row forth, Noah, whither thou list And get thee a new wife.
NOAH	Shem, son, lo, thy mother is wrath. Forsooth, such another I do not know.
SHEM	Father, I shall fetch her in, I vow, Without any fail.

(*Shem goes to his mother*)

SHEM	Mother, my father after thee sends And bids thee into yonder ship wend. Look up and see the wind, For we be ready to sail.

NOAH'S WIFE	Son, go again to him and say I will not come therein today.
NOAH	Come in, wife, in twenty devils' way! Or else stay there without.
HAM	Shall we all fetch her in?
NOAH	Yea, sons, in Christ's blessing and mine, I would you hied you betime, For of this flood I am in doubt.
GOSSIP I	The flood comes in, full fleeting fast, On every side it spreadeth full far, For fear of drowning I am aghast. Good gossip, let us draw near.
GOSSIP II	And let us drink ere we depart, For oftentimes we have done so, For at a draught thou drinkest a quart, And so will I do, ere I go.

(The children go to their mother)

JAPHET	Mother, we pray you all together, For we are here, your own children, Come into the ship for fear of the weather, For his love that you bought.
NOAH'S WIFE	That will I not for all your call Unless I have my gossips all.
SHEM	In faith, mother, yet you shall Whether you will or not.

(The children carry her into the ark)

NOAH	Welcome, wife, into this boat.
NOAH'S WIFE	And have thou that for thy nut!

(She gives him a slap)

NOAH	Aha! Marry, this is hot! It is good to be still.

Irish myth has its own contribution to make to the story:

The Best and Worst Nail in the Ark

The shipwright who made the Ark left empty a place for a nail in it, because he was sure that he himself would not be taken into it. When Noah went into the Ark with his children, as the angel had told him, Noah shut the windows of the Ark and raised his hand to bless it. Now the Devil had come into the Ark along with him as he went into it, and when Noah blessed the Ark the Devil found no other way but the empty hole which the shipwright had left unclosed, and he went into it in the form of a snake; and because of the tightness of the hole he could not go out nor come back, and he was like this until the Flood ebbed; and that is the best and the worst nail that was in the Ark.

Many writers of recent times have written on this story, and here are six examples:

Captain Noah and his Floating Zoo

The Lord looked down on the earth and it made him sad;
'It should have been good what I made but it turned out bad!
There's nothing but sinning, wickedness and violence there,
Remind me to wash Mankind right out of my hair!
I'm gonna make it rain and rain and rain and rain and rain,
I'm gonna make it rain and rain and rain and rain again!
For forty days and forty nights,
'Cos I'm sorry I said "Let there be light"
Rain and rain and rain and rain and rain!

I'm gonna make it rain and rain and rain and rain and rain!
For forty days and nights of rain,
I'm gonna wash those sinners down the drain!
Rain and rain and rain and rain and rain!

But Noah and his family they've been good;
Go Noah, build me an Ark of gopher wood;

Make it four-fifty long, by seventy-five feet wide,
And three decks tall with a roof and a door in the side;
'Cos—
I'm gonna make it rain and rain and rain and rain and rain!
And then I'm gonna make it rain and rain and rain and rain again!
If you want another tip, then here you are:—
Better seal it all up with a good grade tar!
Rain and rain and rain and rain and rain!

When the Ark is finished, here is what you have to do:
You fill it with animals, yes, with animals two by two;
For forty days and forty nights,
Soon there won't be another living soul in sight!
Rain and rain and rain and rain and rain!
'Cos I'm gonna make it
Rain and rain and rain and rain and rain,
And then I'm gonna make it
Rain and rain and rain and rain and rain!
I'm gonna make it rain and rain and rain and rain,
Rain, rain, rain and rain,
I'm gonna make it rain and rain and rain and rain!'

The people of Fun-City, when they couldn't sin no more,
Would go on down to Noah's place, to laugh at poor old Noah.
'You'll never make it float', they jeered,
'You're miles from any shore!'
'So God knows what you're doing!'
'He does indeed,' said Noah.

'Noah! Noah!
Don't do any more,
Look out, man, there's a shark!
Oh ship, ahoy! There, Sailor Boy!'
But he went on building the Ark,
Noah went on building the Ark.

Now Shem, and Ham, and Japhet, they were the sons of Noah;
He made them get all kinds of food and lay them in the store;
Said Mrs Noah, 'Ten thousand buns! What do we need them for?
Enough to feed an Elephant!' 'Enough for two!' said Noah.
 'Noah! Noah!
 Don't do any more,
 Your boat's a laughing stock!
 Ha, ha!'
 But Noah went right on building the Ark,
  And his hammer went knock, knock, knock,
  Noah's hammer went knock, knock, knock.
Then Noah told his sons to do all that the Lord had planned,
To fetch him every kind of thing that's living on dry land;
The ones you see down on the farm, the ones you see in zoos,
All reptiles, birds and insects too, and line them up in twos—
 'Noah! Noah!
 Don't do any more!'
 All the dogs began to bark:
 'Just hark at him, old Jungle Jim!'
 But he went on building the Ark,
 Noah went on building the Ark.

Then Japhet, Shem and Ham,
Fetched a ewe-sheep and a ram,
Duck and drake and bull and cow and cock and hen,
Male and female spotted cheetahs,
Armadillos and ant-eaters,
And mosquit*ers* and two lions from their den.

All the cats and other felines,
Wombats, walruses and sea-lions,
Hippopotami and spiders and gnus,
Bears and bees and golden eagles,
Horses, harvest mice and seagulls,
Apes and humming birds, and worms and kangaroos.

All marsupials and mammals,
Such as wallabies and camels,
Snakes and centipedes, a pair of every one,
They got stuck with one giraffe,
Till they found his better half,
Then from antelope to zebra it was done.

Yes, every living creature,
That walks upon this earth,
Or creeps upon its belly on the land,
Or flies up in the air,
Just you name it, it was there,
It's one pair of each, just as the Lord had planned!

'Noah! Noah! Don't do any more!'
Said the people: 'What a lark!'
As creatures came by every name,
And he led them into the Ark,
Noah led them into the Ark.

With Mrs Shem, and Mrs Ham, and Mrs Japhet too,
And Mrs Noah and their husbands four
They went in two by two.
'Is every living creature there, before I shut the door?
Are you all aboard?'
Inquired the Lord,
'We're all aboard' said Noah.
NOAH! NOAH! You can't do any more!
The skies are getting dark.
The Lord will bring you safe to shore
When you sail away in the Ark.

Michael Flanders

The Ballad of Mrs Noah

Mrs Noah in the Ark
wove a great nightgown out of the dark,
did Mrs Noah,
had her own hearth in the Holy Boat,
two cats, two books, two cooking pots,
had Mrs Noah,
two pints of porter, two pecks of peas,
and a stir in her stew of memories.

Oh, that was a town, said Mrs Noah,
that the Lord in his wrath
did up and drown!

I liked its windows and I liked its trees.
Save me a little Lord, I prayed on my knees.
And now, Lord save me, I've two of each!
apple, apricot, cherry and peach.

How shall I manage it? I've two of them all—
hairy, scaly, leathery, slick,
fluttery, buttery, thin and thick,
shaped like a stick, shaped like a ball,
too tiny to see, and much too tall.

I've all that I asked for and more and more,
windows and chimneys, and a great store
of needles and pins, of outs and ins,
and a regular forgive-us for some of my sins.

She wove a great nightgown out of the dark
decorated like a Sunday Park
with clouds of black thread to remember her grief
sewn about with bright flowers to give relief,
and, in a grim humour, a border all round
with the little white bones of the wicked drowned.

Tell me, Brother, what do you see?
said Mrs Noah to the lowly Worm.

O Mother, the Earth is black, black.
To my crawly bride and lowly me

the Earth is bitter as can be
where the Dead lie down and never come back,
said the blind Worm.

Tell me, Brother, what do *you* see?
said Mrs Noah to the sleeping Cat.

O Mother, the weather is dreadful wet.
I'll keep house for you wherever you'll be.
I'll sit by the fireside and be your pet.
And as long as I'm dry I'll purr for free,
said the snug-loving Cat.

Tell me, Brother, has the Flood gone?
said Mrs Noah to the searching Crow.

No. No. No home in sight.
I fly through the frightful waste alone,
said the carrion Crow.
The World is an everlasting Night.

Now that can't be true, Noah, Old Noah, said
the good Housewife to her good Spouse.

How long must we go on in this floating House?
growing old and hope cold,
Husband, without new land?

And then Glory-Be with a Rainbow to-boot!
the Dove returned with an Olive Shoot.

Tell me, Brother, what have we here,
my Love? to the Dove said Mrs Noah.

It's a Branch of All-Cheer
you may wear on your nightgown all the long year
as a boa, Mrs Noah, said the Dove,
with God's Love!

Then out from the Ark
in her nightgown all dark
with only her smile to betoken the day
and a wreath-round of Olive leaves

Mrs Noah stepped down
into the same old wicked repenting
Lord-Will-We-Ever recently recovered
comfortable World-Town.

O where have you been, Mother Noah, Mother Noah?
I've had a great promise for only Tomorrow.
In the Ark of Sleep I've been on a sail
over the wastes of the world's sorrow.

And the promise? the Tomorrow? Mother Noah,
  Mother Noah?

Ah! the Rainbow's awake
and we will not fail!

Robert Duncan

Noah

They gathered around and told him not to do it,
They formed a committee and tried to take control,
They cancelled his building permit and they stole
His plans. I sometimes wonder he got through it.
He told them wrath was coming, they would rue it,
He begged them to believe the tides would roll,
He offered them passage to his destined goal,
A new world. They were finished and he knew it.
All to no end.
              And then the rain began.
A spatter at first that barely wet the soil,
Then showers, quick rivulets lacing the town,
Then deluge universal. The old man
Arthritic from his years of scorn and toil
Leaned from the admiral's walk and watched them drown.

Roy Daniells

'Twas when the Rain fell Steady

'Twas when the rain fell steady an' the Ark was pitched an' ready
  That Noah got his orders for to take the bastes below;
He dragged them all together by the horn an' hide an' feather,
  An' all excipt the Donkey was agreeable to go.

First Noah spoke him fairly, thin talked to sevairely,
  An' thin he cursed him squarely to the glory av the Lord:—
'Divil take the ass that bred you, and the greater ass that fed you!
  'Divil go wid ye, ye spalpeen!' an' the Donkey wint aboard.

But the wind was always failin', an' 'twas most onaisy sailin',
  An' the ladies in the cabin couldn't stand the stable air;
An' the bastes betwuxt the hatches, they tuk an' died in batches,
  Till Noah said: 'There's wan av us that hasn't paid his fare!'

For he heard a flusteration 'mid the bastes av all creation—
  The trumpetin' av elephints an' bellowin' av whales;
An' he saw forninst the windy whin he wint to stop the shindy
  The Divil wid a stable-fork bedivillin' their tails.

The Divil cursed outrageous, but Noah said umbrageous:
  'To what am I indebted for this tenant-right invasion?'
An' the Divil gave for answer: 'Evict me if you can, sir,
  'For I came in wid the Donkey—on Your Honour's invitation!'

Rudyard Kipling

The Ark

Nobody knows just how they went.
They certainly went in two by two,
But who preceded the kangaroo
And who dared follow the elephant?

'I've had enough,' said Mrs Noah.
'The food just won't go round,' she said.
A delicate deer raised up his head
As if to say, '*I* want no more.'

In they marched and some were sick.
All very well for those who could be
On the rough or the calm or the middle sea.
But I must say that ark felt very thick

Of food and breath. How wonderful
When the dove appeared and rested upon
The hand of Noah. All fear was gone,
The sea withdrew, the air was cool.

Elizabeth Jennings

Noah and the Rabbit

'No land,' said Noah,
'There-is-not-any-land.
Oh, Rabbit, Rabbit, can't you understand?'

But Rabbit shook his head:
'Say it again,' he said;
'And slowly, please.
No good brown earth for burrows,
And no trees;
No wastes where vetch and rabbit-parsley grows,
No brakes, no bushes and no turnip rows,
No holt, no upland, meadowland or weald,
No tangled hedgerow and no playtime field?'

'No land at all—just water,' Noah replied,
And Rabbit sighed.
'For always, Noah?' he whispered, 'will there be
Nothing henceforth for ever but the sea?
Or will there come a day
When the green earth will call me back to play?'

Noah bowed his head:
'Some day . . . some day,' he said.

Hugh Chesterman

Every living creature
an A–Z of beasts and birds

Two of every kind he chose, male and female, perfect, without scar or sore, and they gathered towards the fields of Noah, creeping, flying, running or burrowing through the earth.

Peter Dickinson

35

A Albatross

O Albatross,
following with huge wing-beat
our lonely ship
far from your southern seas,
have you come to haunt some modern mariner
or is it simply company you seek?

Anthony Stuart

Ant

Black is his colour
And he comes out of darkness
To a space of light
Where the grass rattles
And the wind booms.

In his home underground
The stones are silent
Roots and seeds make no noise.

Like fine wires
His legs tremble
Over the ground.

Raindrops hiss and explode
Around him
But he runs zig-zagging
From their cold touch.

At last one raindrop,
Bright balloon of water,
Bursts on his back
Becoming his own flood.
Frantic, he spins,
Finds ground again, and scurries
Towards some crack in an enormous Ark.

Zoë Bailey

A Blackbird Singing

It seems wrong that out of this bird,
Black, bold, a suggestion of dark
Places about it, there yet should come
Such rich music, as though the notes'
Ore were changed to a rare metal
At one touch of that bright bill.

You have heard it often, alone at your desk
In a green April, your mind drawn
Away from its work by sweet disturbance
Of the mild evening outside your room.

A slow singer, but loading each phrase
With history's overtones, love, joy
And grief learned by his dark tribe
In other orchards and passed on
Instinctively as they are now,
But fresh always with new tears.

R. S. Thomas

The Magnificent Bull

My bull is white like the silver fish in the river
white like the shimmering crane bird on the river bank
white like fresh milk!
His roar is like the thunder to the Turkish cannon on the steep shore.
My bull is dark like the raincloud in the storm.
He is like summer and winter.
Half of him is dark like the storm cloud,
half of him is light like sunshine.
His back shines like the morning star.
His brow is red like the beak of the hornbill.
His forehead is like a flag, calling the people from a distance,
He resembles the rainbow.

I will water him at the river,
With my spear I shall drive my enemies.
Let them water their herds at the well;
the river belongs to me and my bull.
Drink, my bull, from the river; I am here
to guard you with my spear.

Dinka Tribe, Africa

C

The Crow

Flying loose and easy, where does he go
Swaggering in the sky, what does he know,
Why is he laughing, the carrion crow?
Why is he shouting, why won't he sing,
How did he steal them, whom will he bring
Loaves of blue heaven under each wing?

Russell Hoban

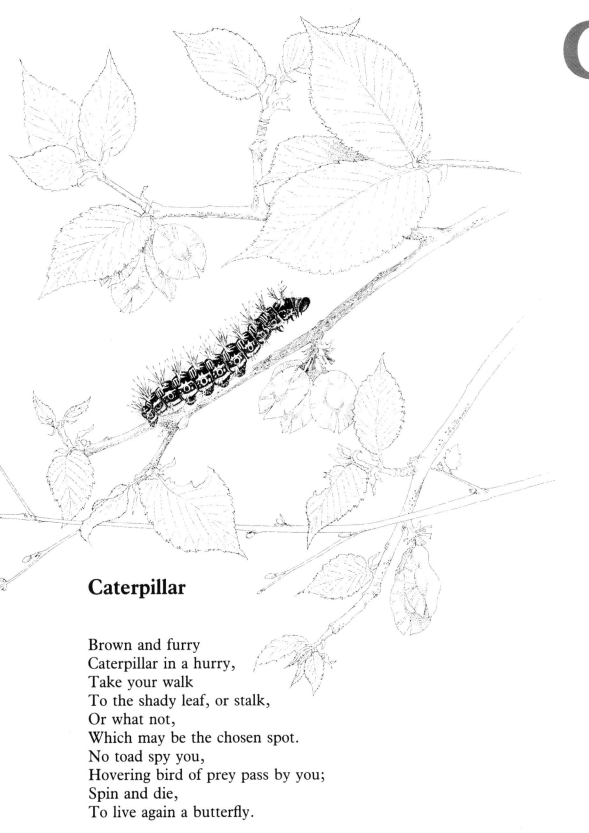

Caterpillar

Brown and furry
Caterpillar in a hurry,
Take your walk
To the shady leaf, or stalk,
Or what not,
Which may be the chosen spot.
No toad spy you,
Hovering bird of prey pass by you;
Spin and die,
To live again a butterfly.

Christina Rossetti

D

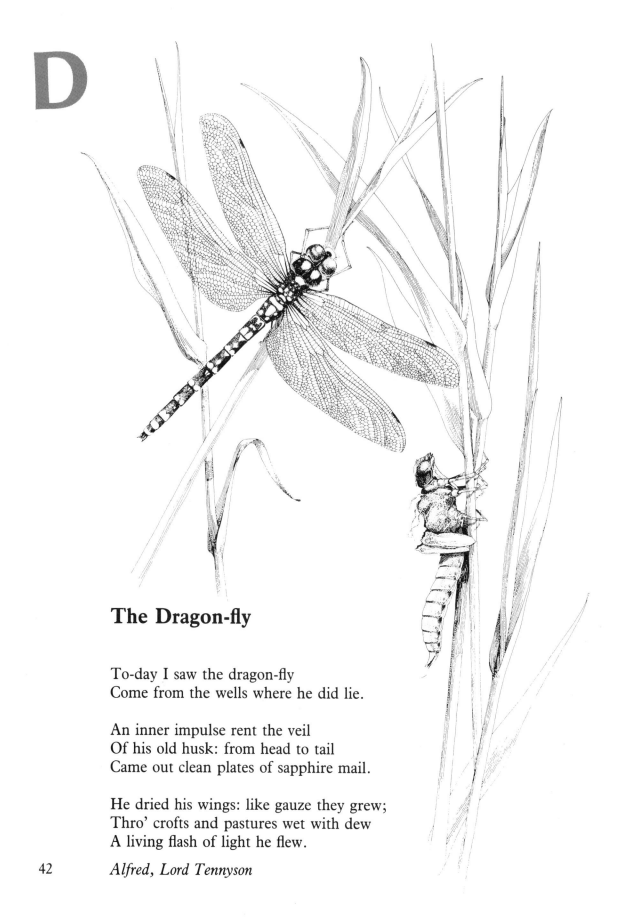

The Dragon-fly

To-day I saw the dragon-fly
Come from the wells where he did lie.

An inner impulse rent the veil
Of his old husk: from head to tail
Came out clean plates of sapphire mail.

He dried his wings: like gauze they grew;
Thro' crofts and pastures wet with dew
A living flash of light he flew.

Alfred, Lord Tennyson

D

The Deers' Request

We are the disappearers.
You may never see us, never,
But if you make your way through a forest
Stepping lightly and gently,
Not plucking or touching or hurting,
You may one day see a shadow
And after the shadow a patch
Of speckled fawn, a glint
Of a horn.
       Those signs mean us.

O chase us never. Don't hurt us.
We who are male carry antlers
Horny, tough, like trees,
But we are terrified creatures,
Are quick to move, are nervous
Of the flutter of birds, of the quietest
Footfall, are frightened of every noise.

If you would learn to be gentle,
To be quiet and happy alone,
Think of our lives in deep forests,
Of those who hunt us and haunt us
And drive us into the ocean.
If you love to play by yourself
Content in that liberty,
Think of us being hunted,
Tell those men to let us be.

Elizabeth Jennings

E

The Eagle

He hangs between his wings outspread
  Level and still
And bends a narrow golden head,
  Scanning the ground to kill,

Though as he sails and smoothly swings
  Round the hill-side,
He looks as though from his own wings
  He hung down crucified.

Andrew Young

Elephant

Elephant
comes last in his loose grey skin. In
the sun you can see brown
hairs on his back. I am sure he
will help to haul the ark
along the flat canal to the flood
when the water has come. He is
not forgetful of all the food
he will need. Have you brought green
leaves, ant-like and prudent elephant?

*Aye, aye, Noah, I have hauled
this tree. It will feed huge me
for a year. Is there space
in the barge?*

George Macbeth

The Windhover

TO CHRIST OUR LORD

I caught this morning morning's minion, king-
   dom of daylight's dauphin, dapple-dawn-drawn falcon, in his riding
   Of the rolling level underneath him steady air, and striding
High there, how he rung upon the rein of a wimpling wing
In his ecstasy! then off, off forth on swing,
   As a skate's heel sweeps smooth on a bow-bend: the hurl and gliding
   Rebuffed the big wind. My heart in hiding
Stirred for a bird,—the achieve of, the mastery of the thing!

Brute beauty and valour and act, oh, air, pride, plume, here
   Buckle! AND the fire that breaks from thee then, a billion
Times told lovelier, more dangerous, O my chevalier!

   No wonder of it: shéer plód makes plough down sillion
Shine, and blue-bleak embers, ah my dear,
   Fall, gall themselves, and gash gold-vermilion.

Gerard Manley Hopkins

Bullfrog

With their lithe long strong legs
Some frogs are able
To thump upon double—
Bass strings though pond-water deadens and clogs.

But you, bullfrog, you pump out
Whole fogs full of horn—a threat
As of a liner looming. True
That, first hearing you
Disgorging your gouts of darkness like a wounded god,
Not utterly fantastical I expected
(As in some antique tale depicted)
A broken-down bull up to its belly in mud,
Sucking black swamp up, belching out black cloud

And a squall of gudgeon and lilies.
                                        A surprise,
To see you, a boy's prize,
No bigger than a rat—all dumb silence
In your little old woman hands.

Ted Hughes

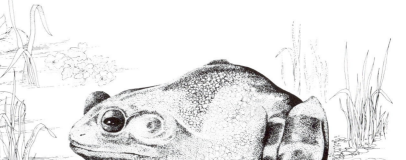

G The Hollow Wood

Out in the sun the goldfinch flits
Along the thistle-tops, flits and twits
Above the hollow wood
Where birds swim like fish—
Fish that laugh and shriek—
To and fro, far below
In the pale hollow wood.

Lichen, ivy, and moss
Keep evergreen the trees
That stand half-flayed and dying,
And the dead trees on their knees
In dog's-mercury and moss:
And the bright twit of the goldfinch drops
Down there as he flits on thistle-tops.

Edward Thomas

G

The Giraffes

I think before they saw me the giraffes
Were watching me. Over the golden grass,
The bush and ragged open tree of thorn,
From a grotesque height, under their lightish horns,
Their eyes were fixed on mine as I approached them.
The hills behind descended steeply: iron-
Coloured outcroppings of rock half covered by
Dull green and sepia vegetation, dry
And sunlit: and above, the piercing blue
Where clouds like islands lay or like swans flew.

Seen from those hills the scrubby plain is like
A large-scale map whose features have a look
Half menacing, half familiar, and across
Its brightness arms of shadow ceaselessly
Revolve. Like a small forked twigs or insects move
Giraffes, upon the great map where they live.

When I went nearer, their long bovine tails
Flicked loosely, and deliberately they turned,
An undulation of dappled grey and brown,
And stood in profile with those curious planes
Of neck and sloping haunches. Just as when,
Quite motionless, they watched I never thought
Them moved by fear, a wish to be a tree,
So as they put more ground between us I
Saw evidence that these were animals
With no desire for intercourse, or no
Capacity.
            Above the falling sun,
Like visible winds the clouds are streaked and spun,
And cold and dark now bring the image of
Those creatures walking without pain or love.

Roy Fuller

Humming Bird

The humming bird refuels
in mid-air from the hub
of a fuchsia flower.
Its belly is feathered white
as rapids; its eye
is smaller than a drop of tar.
A bodied moth, it beats
stopwatches into lethargy
with its wingstrokes.

Food it needs every fifteen
minutes. It has the metabolism
of a steam engine.
Its tiny claws are slight
as pared fingernail;
you could slip it with ease
into a breast pocket.
There it might lie, cowed
—or give you a second heart.

Paul Groves

Hyena

I am waiting for you.
I have been travelling all morning through the bush and not eaten.
I am lying at the edge of the bush
on a dusty path that leads from the burnt-out kraal.
I am panting, it is midday, I found no water-hole.
I am very fierce without food and although my eyes
are screwed to slits against the sun
you must believe I am prepared to spring.

What do you think of me?
I have a rough coat like Africa.
I am crafty with dark spots
like the bush tufted plains of Africa.
I sprawl as a shaggy bundle of gathered energy
like Africa sprawling in its waters.
I trot, I lope, I slaver, I am a ranger.
I hunch my shoulders. I eat the dead.

Do you like my song?
When the moon pours hard and cold on the veldt
I sing, and I am the slave of darkness.
Over the stone walls and the mud walls and the ruined places
and the owls, the moonlight falls.
I sniff a broken drum. I bristle. My pelt is silver.
I howl my song to the moon—up it goes.
Would you meet me there in the waste places?

It is said I am a good match
for a dead lion. I put my muzzle
at his golden flanks, and tear. He
is my golden supper, but my tastes are easy.
I have a crowd of fangs, and I use them.
Oh and my tongue—do you like me
when it comes lolling out of my jaw
very long, and I am laughing?
I am not laughing.
But I am not snarling either, only
panting in the sun, showing you
what I grip
carrion with.

I am waiting
for the foot to slide,
for the heart to seize,
for the leaping sinews to go slack,
for the fight to the death to be fought to the death,
for a glazing eye and the rumour of blood.
I am crouching in my dry shadows
till you are ready for me.
My place is to pick you clean
and leave your bones to the wind.

Edwin Morgan

Ibis

There is a bird called the IBIS. . . .
it enjoys eating corpses or snakes' eggs,
and from such things it takes food home
for its young, which comes most acceptable.
It walks near the seashore by day and night,
looking for little dead fish or other bodies
which have been thrown up by the waves.
It is afraid to enter the water
because it cannot swim.

T. H. White

Ibex

There is an animal called IBEX the Chamois,
which has two horns.
And such is the strength of these that,
if it is hurled down from a high mountain peak
to the very depths,
its whole body will be preserved unhurt
by these two.

T. H. White

The Jackdaw

There is a bird who, by his coat,
And by the hoarseness of his note,
   Might be supposed a crow;
A great frequenter of the church,
Where, bishop-like, he finds a perch,
   And dormitory too.

Above the steeple shines a plate,
That turns and turns, to indicate
   From what point blows the weather.
Look up—your brains begin to swim,
'Tis in the clouds—that pleases him,
   He chooses it the rather.

Fond of the speculative height,
Thither he wings his airy flight,
   And thence securely sees
The bustle and the raree-show
That occupy mankind below,
   Secure and at his ease.

You think, no doubt, he sits and muses
On future broken bones and bruises,
   If he chances to fall.
No; not a single thought like that
Employs his philosophic pate,
   Or troubles it at all.

He sees, that this great roundabout—
The world, with all its motley rout,
   Church, army, physic, law,
Its customs, and its bus'nesses,
Is no concern at all of his,
   And says—what says he?—Caw.

William Cowper

Second Glance at a Jaguar

Skinfull of bowls, he bowls them,
The hip going in and out of joint, dropping the spine
With the urgency of his hurry
Like a cat going along under thrown stones, under cover,
Glancing sideways, running
Under his spine. A terrible, stump-legged waddle
Like a thick Aztec disemboweller,
Club-swinging, trying to grind some square
Socket between his hind legs round,
Carrying his head like a brazier of spilling embers,
And the black bit of his mouth, he takes it
Between his back teeth, he has to wear his skin out,
He swipes a lap at the water-trough as he turns,
Swivelling the ball of his heel on the polished spot,
Showing his belly like a butterfly,
At every stride he has to turn a corner
In himself and correct it. His head
Is like the worn down stump of another whole jaguar,
His body is just the engine shoving it forward,
Lifting the air up and shoving on under,
The weight of his fangs hanging the mouth open,
Bottom jaw combing the ground. A gorged look,
Gangster, club-tail lumped along behind gracelessly,
He's wearing himself to heavy ovals,
Muttering some mantrah, some drum-song of murder
To keep his rage brightening, making his skin
Intolerable, spurred by the rosettes, the cain-brands,
Wearing the spots off from the inside,
Rounding some revenge. Going like a prayer-wheel,
The head dragging forward, the body keeping up,
The hind legs lagging. He coils, he flourishes
The blackjack tail as if looking for a target,
Hurrying through the underworld, soundless.

Ted Hughes

K

The Kingfisher

When Noah left the Ark, the animals
Capered and gambolled on the squadgy soil,
Enjoying their new-found freedom; and the birds
Soared upwards, twittering, to the open skies.
But one soared higher than the rest, in utter ecstasy,
Till all his back and wings were drenched
With the vivid blue of heaven itself, and his breast scorched
With the upward-slanting rays of the setting sun.
When he came back to earth, he had lost the Ark;
His friends were all dispersed. So now he soars no more:
A lonely bird, he darts and dives for fish,
By streams and pools—places where water is—
Still searching, but in vain, for the vanished Ark
And rain-washed terraces of Ararat.

John Heath-Stubbs

Kangaroo

Delicate mother Kangaroo
Sitting up there rabbit-wise, but huge, plumb-weighted,
And lifting her beautiful slender face, oh! so much more gently
 and finely lined than a rabbit's, or than a hare's,
Lifting her face to nibble at a round white peppermint drop
 which she loves, sensitive mother Kangaroo.

Her sensitive, long, pure-bred face.
Her full antipodal eyes, so dark,
So big and quiet and remote having watched so many empty
 dawns in silent Australia.

Her little loose hands, and drooping Victorian shoulders.
And then her great weight below the waist, her vast pale belly
With a thin young yellow little paw hanging out, and straggle
 of a long thin ear, like ribbon,
Like a funny trimming to the middle of her belly, thin little
 dangle of an immature paw, and one thin ear.

D. H. Lawrence

Lapwings

Here come the squealing
clowns
riding the wind.
Baggy wings
trip, flap, flip
out of the sky
over the foam rubber clouds
slap in the face of the
sun.
Black and white sleeves
cartwheel over the trees
and fall
and peel out of a roll
wolf-whistle
and land light on their feet
swank and bow!

Laurence Smith

The Lizard

Lord,
who has inlaid
the triangular throb
of my head
with these thirsting eyes,
and inlaid me
with a flicker quick heart,
please put me
a swift arrow
on a sun-baked wall:
a wall full of cracks,
of mossy havens,
quiet caves of shadow
and hiding places:
a wall alight with joy
and life . . .
let me drink at the fire of Your sky,
until a slit
in the walls of Your paradise
drinks me in, as a trickle of water
dries and is gone.
Amen.

Carmen Bernos de Gasztold
trans. Rumer Godden

Mallard

Squawking they rise from reeds into the sun,
climbing like furies, running on blood and bone,
with wings like garden shears clipping the misty air,
four mallard, hard winged, with necks like rods
fly in perfect formation over the marsh.

Keeping their distance, gyring, not letting slip the air,
but leaping into it straight like hounds or divers,
they stretch out into the wind and sound their horns again.

Suddenly siding to a bank of air unbidden
by hand signal or morse message of command
down sky they plane, sliding like corks on a current,
designed so deftly that all air is advantage,

till, with few flaps, orderly as they left earth,
alighting among curlew they pad on mud.

Rex Warner

Mole

To have to be a mole?

It is like, in a way,
being a little car driven
in the very dark,
                owned
by these endless-
ly tunnelling paws and small
eyes that are good, only,
for the underground.

What can you know of me, this
warm black engine of
busying velvet?

Soft mounds of new, pale
earth like finely-flaked ash
tell you just about where
my country is, but
do you ever see
                      me?

Alan Brownjohn

The Nuthatch

Slate-blue above, buff below,
Descends a tree-trunk upside down,
Punctures a nut with his sharp chisel-bill,
And whistles clear and cheeky,
Shrill as a schoolboy.

John Heath-Stubbs

The Numbat

The numbat
isn't a bat.
OK?
The numbat
looks like a rat.
OK?
It creeps about
using its snout
to eat the ants he
thinks he'd fancy.

If you look for it
in England,
you're sure to meet
with failure,
as the only place
it ever lives
is down in
South Australia.

Michael Rosen

Owls

They stare at you,
these ugly phantoms of the night,
and do not seem to care
if you stare back at them.
All day they perch, half asleep,
in lonely ruins, dark church towers,
not liking the sun,
dozing, and dreaming with stupid face,
of scurrying mice, fat beetles, baby birds,
swallowed greedily in one cruel gulp.

At twilight they come out.
Like floating paper glide along lanes,
noiselessly dipping over hedges,
or fanning their ghostly way
around the houses, down the avenues,
ears and eyes set for the kill.
Then, gorged with fresh meat,
they sag back home,
the moon's eye watching them,
hooting in the wind,
waiting for the next raw victim.

I do not like owls.
I shiver when I hear them
screeching at the bottom of the garden,
invading the darkness,
glad I'm not a mouse,
small bird or beetle.

Leonard Clark

An Otter

    Underwater eyes, an eel's
Oil of water body, neither fish nor beast is the otter:
  Four-legged yet water-gifted, to outfish fish;
    With webbed feet and long ruddering tail
    And a round head like an old tomcat.

    Brings the legend of himself
From before wars or burials, in spite of hounds and verminpoles;
  Does not take root like the badger. Wanders, cries;
    Gallops along land he no longer belongs to;
    Re-enters the water by melting.

    Of neither water nor land. Seeking
Some world lost when first he dived, that he cannot come at since,
  Takes his changed body into the holes of lakes;
    As if blind, cleaves the stream's push till he licks
    The pebbles of the source; from sea

    To sea crosses in three nights
Like a king in hiding. Crying to the old shape of the starlit land,
  Over sunken farms where the bats go round,
    Without answer. Till light and birdsong come
    Walloping up roads with the milk wagon.

Ted Hughes

The Parrots

Somewhere, somewhen I've seen,
But where or when I'll never know,
Three parrots of shrill green
With crests of shriller scarlet flying
Out of black cedars as the sun was dying
Against cold peaks of snow.

From what forgotten life
Of other worlds I cannot tell
Flashes that screeching strife:
Yet the shrill colour and the strident crying
Sing through my blood and set my heart replying
And jangling like a bell.

Wilfred Gibson

On The Porcupine

But O! what Monster's this that bids me battle,
On whose rough back an Host of Pikes doth rattle,
Who string-less shoots so many arrows out,
Whose thorny sides are hedged round about
With stiff steel-pointed quills, and all his parts
Bristled with Bodkins, armed with Awls and Darts,
Which aye fierce darting, seem still fresh to spring,
And to his aid still new supplies to bring?
O fortunate Shaft-never-wanting Bowman!
Who, as thou fleest, can hit thy following foe-man,
And never missest (or but very narrow)
The intended mark of thy self's kindred Arrow:
Who, still self-furnished, needest borrow never
Diana's shafts, nor yet Apollo's quiver,
Nor bow-strings fetched from Carian Aleband,
Brazell from Peru; but hast all at hand
Of thine own growth; for in thy Hide do grow
Thy String, thy Shafts, thy Quiver and thy Bow.

Joshua Sylvester

Quail's Nest

I wandered out one rainy day
And heard a bird with merry joys
Cry 'wet my foot' for half the way;
I stood and wondered at the noise,

When from my foot a bird did flee—
The rain flew bouncing from her breast—
I wondered what the bird could be,
And almost trampled on her nest.

The nest was full of eggs and round;
I met a shepherd in the vales,
And stood to tell him what I found.
He knew and said it was a quail's,

For he himself the nest had found,
Among the wheat and on the green,
When going on his daily round,
With eggs as many as fifteen.

Among the stranger birds they feed,
Their summer flight is short and low;
There's very few know where they breed,
And scarcely any where they go.

John Clare

Quokka and Quoll

Please do not confuse us two
If you should see us in the undergrowth
In our different corners of Australia.
Australia, the Ark that drifted off
With a load of us marsupials aboard.

I am Quokka. Like a large rat
But with a furry tail. Foxes have
Savaged my tribe. I cower now
In sanctuaries—Rottnest, Bald Island—
Eating plants in my tunnelled maze.

I am Quoll. White spots on my fur:
Pretty marsupial pussy. I hunt
Savagely at night. Of my two dozen
Young, only six can suck the milk
In my pouch; the rest must die.

Please do not confuse us, though
We were both saved to suffer slaughter.

Michael Richards

R

Robin Redbreast

You are a strange bird,
a little bundle of contradictions.

If I come near where you peck for food
near the house in the frosted garden,
you do not flit away into the bushes,
you welcome me with song,
you are my friend;
let another bird invade your territory,
you drive him away in anger.

You make your bulky nest in winter,
weaving it beautifully, grasses, wool and moss,
choosing sometimes a hole in a wall,
but as often an old kettle, end of a drain,
even setting up house in church,
lay five or six speckled eggs;
other birds wait for the spring.

And for your pocket size,
what a loud singer you are,
sharp, clear notes
cutting the silences when late afternoon
dims into misted twilight.

Of all birds, the most eccentric.

Leonard Clark

Rat

Rat
leaves a sinking ship. Wise
brown rat, is there blame in that?
If you have to leave the
ark you must oar your way out
with an ant and a ladybird
aloft on your snout. Rat, make a
ring, be a lifebelt here.
And gnaw me a porthole or two
to see through. That will keep you quiet.

> *Rough Noah, I will not. I prefer*
> *a biscuit. And as for sinking,*
> *why it doesn't bear thinking. I*
> *will nip your ankle if you nag at me.*

George Macbeth

The Swan

Silent is my dress when I step across the earth,
reside in my house, or ruffle the waters.
Sometimes my adornments and this high windy air
lift me over the livings of men,
the power of the clouds carries me far
over all people. My white pinions
resound very loudly, ring with a melody,
sing out clearly, when I sleep not on
the soil or settle on grey waters—a travelling spirit.

Anglo-Saxon Riddle
translated by Kevin Crossley-Holland

The Snake Song

Neither legs nor arms have I
But I crawl on my belly
And I have
Venom, venom, venom!

Neither horns nor hoofs have I
But I spit with my tongue
And I have
Venom, venom, venom!

Neither bows nor guns have I
But I flash fast with my tongue
And I have
Venom, venom, venom!

Neither radar nor missiles have I
But I stare with my eyes
And I have
Venom, venom, venom!

I master every movement
For I jump, run and swim
And I spit
Venom, venom, venom!

John Mbiti

Thrushes

Tossed on the glittering air they soar and skim,
Whose voices make the emptiness of light
A windy palace. Quavering from the brim
Of dawn, and bold with song at edge of night,
They clutch their leafy pinnacles and sing
Scornful of man, and from his toils aloof
Whose heart's a haunted woodland whispering;
Whose thoughts return on tempest-baffled wing;
Who hears the cry of God in everything,
And storms the gate of nothingness for proof.

Siegfried Sassoon

Tigress

She grin-lifts
Her black lips and white whiskers
As she yearns forward

Complaining
Tearing complaint off and banging it down a long pipe
That echoes and hums after

Her stride floats
Enjoying a weightlessness
A near-levitation

Again her cry
Scours out the drum of her

Her face
Works at its lacks and longings and quells
Its angers and rehearses its revenges
Endlessly

She lifts again
The welded and bolted plates of her head
Like an illness past curing

She rolls groaning
A bullet of anguish out of her

She is moving, in her hanging regalia
Everything in her is moving, slipping away forward
From the hindward-taper, drawing herself
Out of the air, like a tail out of water

A bow on the war-path, carrying itself
With its dazzling and painted arrows

Shoulders walling her chest, she goes
Between travelling armed walls

Lifting her brow as she walks to ripple
The surface of the element she moves in

Her cry rips the top off the air first
Then disembowels it

She lies down, as if she were lowering
A great snake into the ground

She rests her head on her forepaws, huge trouble
All her lines too enormous for her

I look into her almond eyes. She frowns
Them shut, the fur moving down on her brows.

Ted Hughes

Upupa

There is a bird called the UPUPA, or Hoopoe,
which, when it sees that its parents are growing elderly,
preens their feathers for them, keeps them warm
and licks their eyes.
Thus the parents feel restored.
It looks as if it were saying to its father and mother:
'Just as you worked hard to nourish me,
I am going to do the same for you'.

T. H. White

Ursus

Ursus the Bear, connected with the word 'Orsus' (a beginning),
is said to get her name
because she sculptures her brood with her mouth ('ore').
For they say that these creatures produce a formless foetus,
giving birth to something like a bit of pulp,
and this the mother bear arranges into the proper legs and arms
by licking it. . . .

A bear's head is feeble:
the greatest strength is in the arms and loins,
for which reason they sometimes stand upright.

Nor do they neglect the healer's art. Indeed,
if they are afflicted with a serious injury and damaged by wounds,
they know how to doctor themselves
by stroking their sores with a herb
whose name is Flomus, as the Greeks call it,
so that they are cured by the mere touch.

A sick bear eats ants.

T. H. White

V

Vulture

On ragged black sails
he soars hovering over
everything and death;
a blight in the eye
of the stunning sun.

An acquisitive droop
of beak, head and neck
dangles, dully angling,
a sentient pendulum
next to his keeled chest.

His eyes peer, piously
bloodless and hooded,
far-sighted, blighting
grasses, trees, hill-passes,
stones, streams, bones—ah, bones—

with the tacky slack
of flesh adherent.
A slow ritual fold
of candid devil's palms
in blasphemous prayer—

the still wings sweep closed—
the hyena of skies
plummets from the pulpit
of a tall boredom,
swallowing as he falls.

He brakes lazily
before his back breaks
to settle on two
creaky final wing beats
flinging twin dust-winds.

He squats once fearfully.
Flushed with unhealthy plush
and pregustatory
satisfaction, head back,
he jumps lumpishly up.

Slack neck with the pecked
skin thinly shaking, he
sidles aside then stumps
his deliberate banker's
gait to the stinking meal.

Douglas Livingstone

The Vixen

Among the taller wood with ivy hung,
The old fox plays and dances round her young.
She snuffs and barks if any passes by
And swings her tail and turns prepared to fly.
The horseman hurries by, she bolts to see,
And turns agen, from danger never free.
If any stands she runs among the poles
And barks and snaps and drives them in the holes.
The shepherd sees them and the boy goes by
And gets a stick and progs the hole to try.
They get all still and lie in safety sure,
And out again when everything's secure,
And start and snap at blackbirds bouncing by
To fight and catch the great white butterfly.

John Clare

Woodpecker

Woodpecker is rubber-necked
   But has a nose of steel.
He bangs his head against the wall
   And cannot even feel.

When Woodpecker's jack-hammer head
   Starts up its dreadful din
Knocking the dead bough double dead
   How do his eyes stay in?

Pity the poor dead oak that cries
   In terrors and in pains
But pity more Woodpecker's eyes
   And bouncing rubber brains.

Ted Hughes

Wolf

The Iron Wolf, the Iron Wolf

Stands on the world with jagged fur.
The rusty Moon rolls through the sky.
The iron river cannot stir.
The iron wind leaks out a cry

Caught in the barbed and iron wood.
The Iron Wolf runs over the snow
Looking for a speck of blood.
Only the Iron Wolf shall know

The iron of his fate.
He lifts his nose and moans,
Licks the world clean as a plate
And leaves his own bones.

Ted Hughes

Xestobium nifovillosum

Xestobium nifovillosum
bangs his head
on the floor of his burrow.
The superstitious hearer
thinks death is coming.
In the quiet of the night
as you watch by the dying
you hear the ticking of
the death watch beetle.

Michael Richards

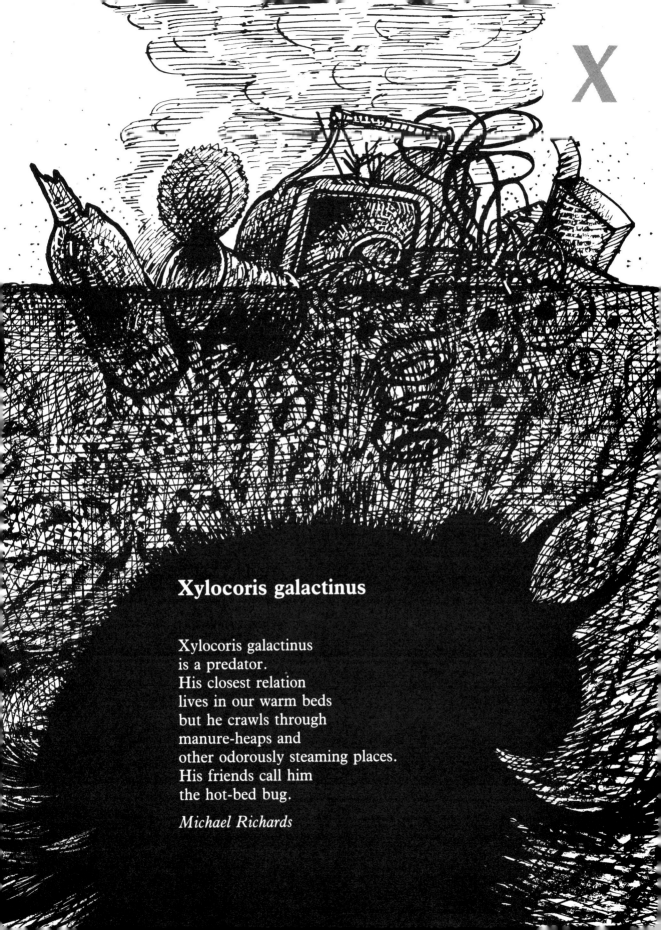

Xylocoris galactinus

Xylocoris galactinus
is a predator.
His closest relation
lives in our warm beds
but he crawls through
manure-heaps and
other odorously steaming places.
His friends call him
the hot-bed bug.

Michael Richards

The Yellowhammer

When shall I see the white-thorn leaves agen,
   And yellowhammers gathering the dry bents
By the dyke-side, on stilly moor or fern,
   Feathered with love and nature's good intents?
Rude is the tent this architect invents,
   Rural the place, with cart ruts by dyke side.
Dead grass, horse hair, and downy-headed bents
   Tied to dead thistles—she doth well provide,
Close to a hill of ants where cowslips bloom
   And shed o'er meadows for their sweet perfume.
In early spring, when winds blow chilly cold,
   The Yellowhammer, trailing grass, will come
To fix a place and choose an early home,
   With yellow breast and head of solid gold.

John Clare

The Mad Yak

I am watching them churn the last milk
 they'll ever get from me.
They are waiting for me to die;
They want to make buttons out of my bones.
Where are my sisters and brothers?
That tall monk there, loading my uncle,
 he has a new cap.
And that idiot student of his—
I never saw that muffler before.
Poor uncle, he lets them load him.
How sad he is, how tired!
I wonder what they'll do with his bones?
And that beautiful tail!
How many shoelaces will they make of that!

Gregory Corso

Z Zebra Finch

When the sun is high
the shadows of the leaves are dark,
the patches between are bright.

In and out the air
beneath the leaves
flies the bird you cannot see.

The white light and the leaves' shadows
make its feathers.
All you see
is the shape of a moving leaf.

Michael Rosen

The Zebras

From the dark woods that breathe of fallen showers,
Harnessed with level rays in golden reins,
The zebras draw the dawn across the plains
Wading knee-deep among the scarlet flowers.
The sunlight, zithering their flanks with fire,
Flashes between the shadows as they pass
Barred with electric tremors through the grass
Like wind along the gold strings of a lyre.

Into the flushed air snorting rosy plumes
That smoulder round their feet in drifting fumes,
With dove-like voices call the distant fillies,
While round the herds the stallion wheels his flight,
Engine of beauty volted with delight,
To roll his mare among the trampled lilies.

Roy Campbell

God loosed the rain

God loosed the rain. And more than rain. He loosed the under seas upon the land.

Peter Dickinson

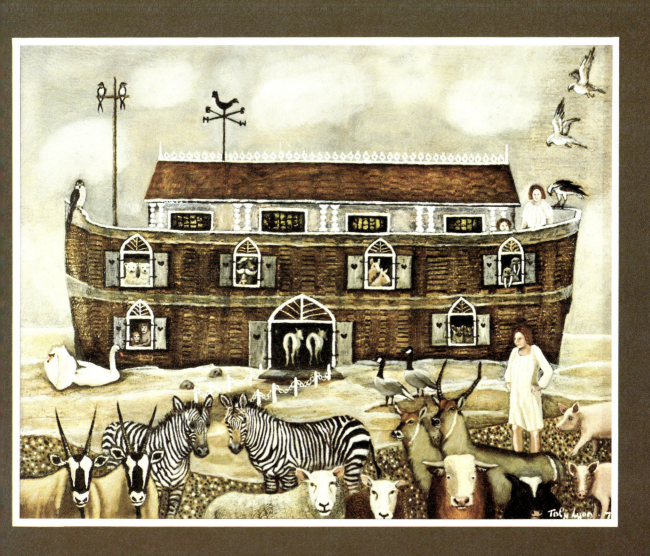

The Miracle Play *continues*

NOAH   Ah, children, methinks my boat removes
Our tarrying here hugely me grieves
Over the land the water spreads.
God do as he will.

This window will I shut anon
And into my chamber will I gone
Till this water, so great one
Be slacked through thy might.

ALL   Save me, O God; for the waters are come in unto my soul.
I sink in deep mire, where there is no standing:
I am come into deep waters, where the floods overflow me.
Deliver me out of the mire, and let me not sink: let me be delivered from them that hate me, and out of the deep waters.
Let not the waterflood overflow me, neither let the deep swallow me up, and let not the pit shut her mouth upon me.

Captain Noah and his Floating Zoo *continues*

It looks like rain,
Now won't that just be jolly!
It looks like rain,
You know I thought it would.
It looks like rain,
I must go and get my brolly,
A short sharp shower
Will do the flowers good.

It looks like rain,
In fact it's really pouring;
It looks like rain,
The ground has turned to mud!
It looks like rain,
Can you hear the river roaring!
I shouldn't be surprised if it was going to flood!

And now it's round my ankles,
And now it's round my knees;
And some are on the roof tops,
And some are climbing trees!
OH GOD FORGIVE ME PLEASE!

It looks like the sea
Is rising like a fountain,
It looks like HELP!
I'm making for the mountain
It looks like AHH!
The world's a brimming jug!
The water's round my shoulders, and I'm
GLUG! GLUG! GLUG!

For the floodgates of Heaven were opened
And the springs of the deep broke through,
And the waters went on rising
As the Lord did command them to.
Then all things living and breathing
On the face of the earth did drown,
For even the peaks of the mountains
Were a good five fathoms down, way down,
A good five fathoms down.
But the Lord he remembered his promise
And the Ark went floating free,
And the hope of the world went with it,
As it sailed on that endless sea.

Forty days and nights—living under hatches,
Careful with the lights—feed the beasts in batches;
And I can't hear them roar as they're waiting to be fed,
For the rain's steady drumming on the roof above my head,
The raindrops drumming overhead.

Here inside the Ark—rolling, pitching, turning,
Everything is dark—no more oil for burning,
And I just can't breathe, and my feet are made of lead;
And the rain's steady drumming on the roof above my head,
The raindrops drumming overhead.

Forty days at sea—how the timbers shudder!
God has promised me he will be our rudder;
But I hope he won't hear, when I wish that I were dead!
With the rain's steady drumming on the roof above my head,
The raindrops drumming overhead.

Michael Flanders

Rain

Rain
is the one who goes on. He is flung
pita-pata-pita-pata from a
tipped bowl of dry peas. Wet fur,
wet wood, wet wings, wet canvas: the
whole wide world is awash in a
sluice of beans. Rattle, rush.
Down comes the roof in a slush
of cold glass bits. Below decks
glum beasts peer out and steam dry slowly.

I pour in. Always in
motion, a flow in the air, I
slither to all points. And fill earth
top-full of water, of water, of water.

George Macbeth

Then died the corrupted beasts

Then died the corrupted beasts also, the winged lions and the sphinxes, the dragons and the unicorns, and none was ever seen again.

Peter Dickinson

Deinosaurs

I love the Deinosaurs, their padded bulk,
Their little heads, so clearly made to sulk,
Their decorative ridges, and each plate
Of armour, so fantastic, big and blate
I like its overlapping—how they must
Have lumbered, moving under all that crust,
Immortal pies, and nourished, if they could,
Those craving guts, so long before the Flood.

I like the Brontosaurus, with his tail
Busy among the saplings like a flail,
His long long back, his hundred feet of span.
So much more satisfying than mere man.
How long it must have taken for a pin
Stuck in his tail, to send its message in!
I like his jointed neck that could uprear
Some forty feet, and round the parish peer,
A useful friend to have, a sentinel,
A mower, roller, for the lawn as well,
A gentle creature, like a donkey or
A camel—such a harmless deinosaur.

I like the Stegosaurus even now,
Though one would scarcely harness *him* to plough
He had his points—at least life was not dull.
When he was prowling for his bellyfull.
They must, in their own heavyfooted way,
Have made the most of their Jurassic day;
Even their loves, had one been there to see,
Would have made conversation over tea;
I should have beat it when Triceratops
And loving partner, had their Combined Ops.
And two Tyrannosauri would have made
A pretty havoc in some bowery glade!

Arthur J. Bull

Dragon Night

Little flame mouths,
Cool your tongues.
Dreamtime starts,
My furnace lungs.

Rest your wings now,
Little flappers,
Cave mouth calls
To dragon nappers.

Night is coming,
Bank your fire.
Time for dragons
To retire.

Hiss.
Hush.
Sleep.

Jane Yolen

The Unicorn

All the beasts obeyed Noah when he admitted them into the ark. All but the unicorn. Confident of his own strength, he boasted 'I shall swim.' For forty days and forty nights the rains poured down and the oceans boiled as in a pot and all the heights were flooded. The birds of the air clung onto the ark and when the ark pitched they were all engulfed. But the unicorn kept on swimming. When, however, the birds emerged again they perched on his horn and he went under—and that is why there are no unicorns now.

Ukrainian Folk Tale

The Unicorn

Look hard enough, and you will find,
Cropping the grass and breathing air,
This fancy creature of the mind.

Once he was like an angel, spare,
Light-headed, speedy, blazing white,
And though quite meek with girls, could scare

Their dads, and give the lion a fight;
That's how the stories say he was,
But now, for some bad deed, he's quite

Transformed, begrimed with mud and moss,
With slow wit, thick limbs and bad breath—
A black, bead-eyed rhinoceros!

No girl, no man disputes his path;
He kills the lion, destroys our car,
Puts up a good fight with Jack Death.

And what a change of face! how far
A cry from limbs of fire and light!
Yet, in this bitter world of war,

Of wasted fruit and blunted sight,
Of children starved and kindness torn,
A beastly rhino seems more right

Than the angelic unicorn.

Edward Lowbury

The Coming of the Phoenix Bird

On the banks of the Nile
lies the city of Heliopolis
the city of the sun

and in that city is a place of stone
paved flat and round like a ring.

There, one morning
when the end of time will come
they'll spread live sulphur on the ground
and spices brought from the hills.

The sun will rise, the people will cry
a spark will fall, a flame will rise
out of the sky will fly the Phoenix bird
with a crest of feathers upon his head
his beak as blue as the Indian sea.

With his wings spread like an eagle
and tail spread like a fan
into the fire he will fly
to burn among the spices
for a day and a night through.

There on the stones in the ring
as night turns into day
and the sun fills the sky,
there amongst the ashes
men shall look and find a worm.

On the second day next after
that worm will become Phoenix alive
and on the third after the night of fire
the Phoenix bird will take its ashes up
from the place of fire
and fly with every bird from every bush
back to the sun in the sky.

That is the story of the Phoenix bird
who lives alone in the sun
and dies where he is born.

Michael Rosen

Yet Gentle will the Griffin be

The moon? It is a griffin's egg,
Hatching tomorrow night.
And how the little boys will watch
With shouting and delight
To see him break the shell and stretch
And creep across the sky.
The boys will laugh. The little girls,
I fear, may hide and cry.
Yet gentle will the griffin be,
Most decorous and fat,
And walk up to the Milky Way
And lap it like a cat.

Vachel Lindsay

Noah sends the raven and the dove

For another twenty days Noah waited, and then he opened the little window which God had shown him he must make in the roof and cast one of the ravens up into the sky. . . .
Seven days later he took one of the pigeons and cast it up. . . .

Peter Dickinson

The Miracle Play *continues*

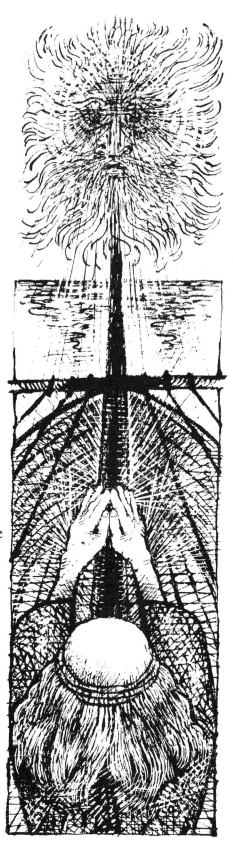

NOAH   Now forty days are fully gone
Send a raven I will anon
If anywhere earth, tree or stone
Be dry in any place.

(He lets a raven fly out of the window)

And if this fowl come not again
It is a sign, sooth to say,
That dry it is on hill or plain,
And God hath done some grace.

Ah, Lord, wherever this raven be,
Somewhere is dry, well I see.
But yet a dove, by my loyalty,
After will I send.

Thou wilt turn again to me,
For of all fowls that can fly
Thou art most meek and kind.

(He lets a dove fly out of the window. It returns, bearing an olive branch)

My sweet dove to me brought has
A branch of olive from some place.
This betokeneth God has done us some grace
And is a sign of peace.

Ah, Lord, blessed be thou aye
That me hast comfort thus today.
By this sight I may well say
This flood begins to cease.

GOD   Noah, take thy wife anon
And thy children every one.
Out of the ship thou shalt gone,
And they all with thee.

Beasts and all that can fly
Out anon they shall hie
On earth to grow and multiply,
I will that it be so.

My rainbow between you and me
In the firmament shall be
By very token that you may see
That such vengeance shall cease.

The string is turned toward you
And toward me is bent the bow
That such weather shall never show
And this I promise thee.

My blessing now I give thee here,
To thee, Noah, my servant dear,
For vengeance shall no more appear.
And now, farewell, my darling dear.

Captain Noah and his Floating Zoo *continues*

Comes another day different from the others;
Shem begins to say something to his brothers,
But his voice stops short:—there's nothing to be said;
The rain isn't drumming on the roof above my head!
The rain's stopped drumming overhead!

For the Lord closed the floodgates of Heaven
And the springs of the deep blue sea.
And he sent a west wind blowing
To dry it up gradually.
The waters slowly subsided
Over many long days and weeks,
'Til one day they were dotted with islands,
The tips of the mountain peaks,
They were the mighty mountain peaks.
The Ark went peacefully floating
And the sea was calm and flat,
'Til the Lord God brought it to rest at last
On the top of Mount Ararat.

Father Noah please open the porthole, let's have a peep at the world
    outside;
Though we thank the Lord who saved us, 'Cain and Abel!'
    What a ride!
Can't believe the Ark's not moving, are we on a mountain top?
We've come down a whole lot lower, I just felt my ears go pop!
Let's have a peep through the porthole, father!
Mother first, then me, then me!
Mrs Shem is so very tiny,
She can't even see the sea!

Father Noah sent forth a raven flapped around and shouted 'Caw';
'Have another try tomorrow'—croaked the raven, 'Never more!'
I can see our tiny island, is it really Ararat?
Let me lean out even further!—There goes Mrs Japhet's hat!
Let's have a peep through the porthole, father!
Mrs Ham must have a shot!
'So you boys can see my bloomers?
Thank you, no! I'd rather not!'
Father sent a dove to look out, circled round, but found no land,
Then it flew right back through the porthole,
Settled safe on father's hand.
Sent the dove again aflying, after waiting for a week,
Back it came that very same evening, an olive twig held in its beak.
Let's have a peep through the porthole, father!
Look at what the dove has found,
Where the olive trees are showing
Soon there's going to be dry ground.

One more week, then off we sent it, waited all that day and then
Sent the other dove to join it, neither one came back again;
Now they need no Ark for shelter,
There the doves will build their nest,
Where the olive trees are growing,
Make their home and take their rest.

Father Noah, please open the hatches,
Now it must be safe to try;
Gaze about us, blinking in the sunlight,
All the earth around is dry:
ALL THE WORLD AROUND IS DRY!

Michael Flanders

Noah's Song

The animals are silent in the hold,
Only the lion coughing in the dark
As in my ageing arms once more I fold
My mistress and the mistress of the Ark.

That, the rain, and the lapping of the sea:
Too many years have brought me to this boat
Where days swim by with such monotony,
Days of the fox, the lion, and the goat.

Her breathing and the slow beat of the clock
Accentuate the stillness of the room,
Whose walls and floor and ceiling seem to lock
Into a space as single as the tomb.

A single room set up against the night,
The hold of animals, and nothing more:
For any further world is out of sight—
There are no people, and there is no shore.

True, the time passes in unbroken peace:
To some, no doubt, this Ark would seem a haven.
But all that I can hope for is release.
Tomorrow I'll send out the dove and raven.

Evan Jones

Raven

Then, as the lifted land lay upwards,
Where the wind and weather warped it,
The ark upon a soft day, settled to the ground,
By a raised up rock, rested it at last,
On the mount of Marrach, on the Armerne hills
Waft Noe his window wide, and wised thereout;
Sought the service of his servants, the earth to seek,
Remembered he the raven, (rank rebel Raven!
O Coloured as a coal! O crow untrue!)
Flaps he into flight, fanning on the wind,
High is he upon his heart, to hearken tidings!
Croaks he for comfort, for carrion he finds,
For cast upon the cliffs the rotting corpses lay.
He smelt the stench, and sought them,
Fell upon the foul flesh, filling full his belly,
Full soon, slips yesterday's strife and storm,
Forgotten his captain's charges, left in the coffer,
The raven recking forth, recks he very little
How all other fare, if he findeth meat!

Anon, 14th Century

The Turtle Dove

One day, one day,
After the eagles of war have preyed,
When the flowers appear on the earth, and it is spring—
The time of the singing of birds—the turtle dove
(As when the first flood-waters fell away)

Will build her nest in the heart of the peaceful grove.

John Heath-Stubbs

Go Little Dove

NOAH   Go little Dove, alone, alone,
Above the cruel flood
And find a crest of slippery stone
Or some small field of mud
To prove that underneath the waves
Are mountains, houses, trees and caves.

ALL   Go little Dove,
Go little Dove.

DOVE   O master, I will fly and fly
Until my wings grow weak
To find some sign beneath the sky
Of what we truly seek.
Believe in me: believe in me
That I may find some hill or tree.

ALL   Go little Dove,
Go little Dove.

ANIMALS   Go little Dove, or we will die,
We're hungry as can be.
Set sail, sweet bird, into the sky
And see what you can see.
For we are frightened and we yearn
For woods and valleys to return.

ALL   Go little Dove,
Go little Dove.

DOVE   (*to mate*) Be not afraid: I will return
And fold you to my breast.
Now let me go, because I burn
With such a sharp unrest.
I cannot wait! Give way! I sail
Into the centre of the gale!

ALL   O little Dove,
O little Dove.

Mervyn Peake

Pigeons

They haunt the garden now, the pair of them—
Grey shapes aground among the risen flowers
As though fast-bound by some invisible cord.
And in the dawn
The muted clatter of their flight breaks through
Grey unawareness; when the first light creeps
Sure as a thief with keys for every room
I hear the silken rattle of their wings.

Now midway across the bridge where the crowds are thick
And traffic hinders every exit, I
Without sight of the river, slowing, blindfolded
Against the bank before my face, am driven
For consolation in the thought of wings
Grey as buildings round a city square,
And things as unexpected as the leaf
Which brought a sudden hope to Noah's eyes.

Surely he stretched his hand
In thankfulness and felt his fears grow slack
As I feel now to hear these pigeons' wings
Breaking the tension this side where we stand
Hindered, and yet directed, losing hope
And finding it outside the charted lines
That rule our numbered days.

Phoebe Hesketh

Noah

When old Noah stared across the floods,
Sky and water melted into one
Looking-glass of shifting tides and sun.

Mountain-tops were few: the ship was foul:
All the morn old Noah marvelled greatly
At this weltering world that shone so stately,
Drowning deep the rivers and the plains.
Through the stillness came a rippling breeze;
Noah sighed, remembering the green trees.

Clear along the morning stooped a bird,—
Lit beside him with a blossomed sprig.
Earth was saved; and Noah danced a jig.

Siegfried Sassoon

The animals leave the ark

All the animals came marching out, orderly as a king's army, and began to scatter along the range seeking new lairs and new pastures.

Peter Dickinson

Captain Noah and his Floating Zoo *continues*

Then,
The Lord looked down on the Ark and he spoke to Noah:
'Come out of the Ark and begin your life once more.
Come out with your wife and your sons and your daughters there,
And set the animals free and the birds of the air.'

And they came out
2 by 2 by 2 by 2 by 2.
Running down the gang-plank—
2 by 2 by 2 by 2 by 2.
The Lord said. 'Go where it suits you best
And cover the earth from east to west,
By 2 by 2 by 2 by 2 by 2.

But dog and cat and ox and ass I give for Noah to keep;
With chicken, turkey, duck and goose, and horse and goat and sheep
And man shall sow and till the ground, and fill it with increase;
While spring shall follow winter round, until the world shall cease.
Though they do evil in my sight, I bless the sons of men,
I'll never send another flood, to wipe them out again;
My pledge shall stand between us, as a sign for all to know,
And when the rainclouds gather
In the sky I'll set my bow . . .'

Oh what a wonderful scene—
The rainbow overhead,
Violet, indigo, blue and green,
Yellow, orange and red.
 'This is my promise to you,—
 The rainbow overhead,
 Violet, indigo, blue and green,
 All the colours that lie between
 Violet, indigo, blue and green,
 Yellow, orange and red.
You'll see the rainbow in the sky,
You'll know God's words are true:
Go forth, increase, and multiply—
BY—
2 by 2 by 2 by 2 by 2 by 2 by 2 by 2 by 2 . . .

Michael Flanders

Disembarkation Chorus

So disembark! The storm has found its ending,
The rains have poured their very selves away,
The rocks are all a-gleaming and a-blending,
And we shall step ashore this very day

On Ararat,
On Ararat,
Sweet Ararat, the golden.

Ashore! ashore! All birds! All flies! All fishes!
And every kind of animal, give way
To Captain Noah, and obey his wishes,
For he has found safe anchorage today

On Ararat,
On Ararat,
Sweet Ararat, the golden.

Praise be to all the Angels and the Voices,
Praise be to this great sun that burns the rain,
Praise be to Rainbows when the heart rejoices
To see the colours of the world again

On Ararat,
On Ararat,
Sweet Ararat, the golden.

Mervyn Peake

Sand

Sand
clutches the keel in his cool
hands. The whole ship
sinks in his soft flesh that
grates to the timbers. Ahoy,
sand. Say, may we step down
and stand on your smooth back?
First comes lynx, is my
look-out. His firm claws
hardly can scar your salt-washed skin.

Yes, you may land. But let
insects come out first. I
must get used to the peck
of your feet, send the small first.

George Macbeth

When the Animals were let out of the Ark after the Flood

There was scurrying and scrimmage when the wild ones all escaped:
Each fowl took to flight, that his feathers would serve,
Each fish to the flood that could use its fins,
Each beast to the fields that feeds on herbs,
Wild worms to their homes wriggle in the earth,
The fox and the pole-cat wend to the wood,
Harts to the high heath, hares to the gorse,
And lions and leopards to the lake-caverns,
Eagles and hawks to the high rocks,
The whole-footed fowl fares to the flood,
And each beast in a bustle to where best he likes.

Anon, 14th Century

The Good Place

Back-along, the forest was a good place;
    An animal could go walk-about
    enjoy sniff-around and show his face
    and howl or bark or mew
    according to his fancy.
There were good neighbours in the trees
—whistling birds and singing birds
and very sociable honeybees,
and little grey monkeys,
and bats and cats and Fabled Things
too glorious for words
—in the forest, when it was a good place.

It began when we left the Ark,
full of goodwill and peanuts,
with Noah beaming through the dark
in-between-time of dawn.
'My life! Good luck! Bon Voyage!' he cried
—a jolly old boy in a red skull-cap;
and we wandered away
into the brand new day
where the wet world lay,
each leading his mate and family,
with Mrs Noah gently weeping
buckets into the old man's beard.

Some took to the trees, creeping
about the green glooms, keeping
very much to themselves, to their kind,
remembering the voyage, the Flood,
the overcrowding, the fish dinners,
the rain shrouding the horizons blind
and everyone moody, except the ducks
—who have water on the mind.
 Then there was the padding about,
 the exploration with ears and snout,
 the luxurious cocking of legs,
 the steady treading of trails.

Some walked, some crawled, some swung by their tails
 beneath the bones of a mackerel shoal
 which gleamed so white on the forest boughs,
 scaring the dogs and the Friesian cows,
 alarming the tigers on their evening prowls,
 tinkling in the owlish breeze
 that hovered under the dripping trees;
 and it was button mushrooms and ripe berries,
 shoots and roots and sweet potatoes,
 nuts and apples and tender bark,
 haws and hips and plump black cherries
 in the good place, back-along.

That's how it began, lots of summers ago
—a roar, a howl and the thrush's song
skirling on the edge of sleep,
the moo of cattle, the baa of sheep,
a dragon's blow-lamp snore,
creatures settling down to keep
each other company,
under the old stars and the old moon
to go no more a-roving
—ox and fox and turkey cocks,
hare and bear and Fabled Thing,
badger, deer and coon-racoon.

   In the good place, back-along,
the hawks clipped their talons,
the tigers sheathed their claws
and were most polite and quiet
on a vegetarian diet
of quagga's milk and haws.
   Sentimental lions
held fox-whelps in their paws
and crooned silly lullabies
to the little bats and little cats
and all the young jackdaws,
because it was a good time and a good place.

Then, and again and again, came Men.
First there came Ham with his bow
and his little piggy eyes and low
forehead and strange desires.
Then there came Shem with his spear,
guzzling beer from a clay pot
and lighting fires and killing an awful lot
of animals and birds—for fun.

So, one by one, we turned away
from all we had learned in the Ark,
back to the burrows and holes and earths,
running in the dark.

That's how it ended.

Brian Carter

Go forth and multiply

Pigeon and Wren

Coo-oo, coo-oo
It's as much as a pigeon can do
    To maintain two;
But the little wren can maintain ten
And bring them up like gentlemen.

Anon

A Crocodile

Hard by the lilied Nile I saw
A duskish river-dragon stretched along,
The brown habergeon of his limbs enamelled
With sanguine almerdines and rainy pearl:
And on his back there lay a young one sleeping,
No bigger than a mouse; with eyes like beads,
And a small fragment of its speckled egg
Remaining on its harmless, pulpy snout;
A thing to laugh at, as it gaped to catch
The baulking, merry flies. In the iron jaws
Of the great devil-beast, like a pale soul
Fluttering in rocky hell, lightsomely flew
A snowy troculus, with roseate beak
Tearing the hairy leeches from his throat.

Thomas Lovell Beddoes

A Lamb

Yes, I saw a lamb where they've built a new housing
estate, where cars are parked in garages, where
streets have names like Fern Hill Crescent

I saw a lamb where television aerials sprout from
chimneypots, where young men gun their motor-
bikes, where mothers watch from windows between
lace curtains

I saw a lamb, I tell you, where lawns in front are
neatly clipped, where cabbages and cauliflowers
grow in back gardens, where doors and gates are
newly painted

I saw a lamb, there in the dusk, the evening fires just
lit, a scent of coal-smoke on the air, the sky faintly
bruised by the sunset

yes, I saw it, I was troubled. I wanted to ask someone
anyone, something, anything . . .

a man in a raincoat coming home from work but he
was in a hurry. I went in at the next gate and rang
the doorbell, and rang, but no one answered.

I noticed that the lights in the house were out. Someone shouted at me from an upstairs window next
door, 'They're on holiday. What do you want?'
And I turned away because I wanted nothing

but a lamb in a green field.

Gael Turnbull

Cow in Calf

It seems she has swallowed a barrel.
From forelegs to haunches
her belly is slung like a hammock.

Slapping her out of the byre is like slapping
a great bag of seed. My hand
tingled as if strapped, but I had to
hit her again and again and
heard the blows plump like a depth-charge
far in her gut.

The udder grows. Windbags
of bagpipes are crammed there
to drone in her lowing.
Her cud and her milk, her heats and her calves
keep coming and going.

Seamus Heaney

The Mare

The mare lies down in the grass where the nest of the skylark is hidden.
Her eyes drink the delicate horizon moving behind the song.
Deep sink the skies, a well of voices. Her sleep is the vessel of Summer.
That climbing music requires the hidden music at rest.

Her body is utterly given to the light, surrendered in perfect abandon
To the heaven above her shadow, still as her first-born day.
Softly the wind runs over her. Circling the meadow, her hooves
Rest in a race of daisies, halted where butterflies stand.

Do not pass her too close. It is easy to break the circle
And lose that indolent fullness rounded under the ray
Falling on light-eared grasses your footstep must not yet wake.
It is easy to darken the sun of her unborn foal at play.

Vernon Watkins

The Thrush's Nest

Within a thick and spreading hawthorn bush
　　That overhung a mole-hill large and round,
I heard from morn to morn a merry thrush
　　Sing hymns to sunrise, while I drank the sound
With joy; and, often an intruding guest,
　　I watched her secret toils from day to day—
How true she warped the moss to form a nest,
　　And modelled it within with wood and clay;
And by and by, like heath-bells gilt with dew,
　　There lay her shining eggs, as bright as flowers,
Ink-spotted over shells of greeny blue;
　　And there I witnessed, in the sunny hours,
A brood of nature's minstrels chirp and fly,
Glad as that sunshine and the laughing sky.

John Clare

Grandpa Bear's Lullaby

The night is long
But fur is deep.
You will be warm
In winter sleep.

The food is gone
But dreams are sweet
And they will be
Your winter meat.

The cave is dark
But dreams are bright
And they will serve
As winter light.

Sleep, my little cubs, sleep.

Jane Yolen

Finale for the Animals

Some with cruelty came, sharp-fanged and clawed,
Tore at the air searching for food which, found,
They ate in an instant—new leaves, the tall and small
Flowers. Carnivores were
Worse, hunters of blood, smellers of victims
More miles away than our instruments measure or we
Imagine. Meanwhile the jungle listened and looked.
The parrot kept its beak shut, the slithering snake
Stilled to a coil. The stars were listening, the sun's
Burning paused at the tear and rampage of
A striped or spotted creature. This was the time
Before we were.

Now we have caged and enclosed but not enchanted
Most of these. Now full of power we are not
Gentle with flowers, pull too hard, break the admired
Rose with abandonment. We should know better.

You have heard of the ark and Noah. Most likely it
Was a local event or a myth but remember men
Bow down to the myths they create.
Perhaps we were kindest, most gentle,
Most at our best
When we coupled all creatures and launched them forth
 in an ark.
Imagination was gracious then indeed,
Gracious too when we thought up the speeding dove,
Feathery emblem of peace whiter than clouds, its wings
Combing and calming the breakers. The waters stilled.

You have heard now of some of these, learnt of their habits.
Do not haunt zoos too often, do not demand
Affection too often from rabbits or cats or dogs,
Do not tame if taming hurts.
Be grateful for such variety of manners,
For the diverse universe.
Above all respect the smallest of all these creatures
As you are awed by the stars.

Elizabeth Jennings

A second flood

Sheila Burnford looks ahead to the possibility of a second flood:

A Second Ark

This would be his last visit, alas, he said, as his office would soon be moving to its new location under the Lunar Colonization Scheme—somewhere near the Crater Tycho, he thought. Seeing that Mr Noah looked puzzled, he explained once more what he had been trying to explain for the last two years if only anyone in the Family would listen. The world was being abandoned: a project similar to Mr Noah's, but on a human scale of course, was already in action. A rocket base had been established on Mount Everest, a computer had selected the best pairs of every possible combination of genes from every human race and occupation, and two by two these selections were entering the thousand-seater spacecraft which left daily at 21.05 hours, non-stop, for the Sea of Tranquillity, where a Lunar Government, administered jointly by the Salvation Army, the Red Cross and the International Union of Teamsters, was already in operation.

The Bank Manager thought Mr Noah would be gratified to hear that the scheme had been named 'Operation Noah' in recognition of the Family's contribution to conservation. Of course there could be no animals in this New World, he went on, but apparently some colonists were already making pets out of synthetically formed bacteria. It had been estimated that by the time the last spacecraft took off, there would be no animals (other than those on the Ark) left behind on the world. Apparently they had been seeing to it themselves over the years that their numbers dwindled in proportion to the land left.

He was full of praise for the way in which every detail of the Scheme had been organized: it was flawless, down to the last doughnut and cup of coffee handed out by the Salvation Army before embarkation. In fact, the only unforeseen difficulty had been the problem of the space litter already in orbit. Sometimes the spacecraft were stacked for weeks awaiting the opportunity to dodge through the rocket cones and other discarded waste of the previous entrants. However, as the tickets were only one way, this would not inconvenience anyone once the last colonist had been landed on the moon.

After the computerized humans had left, it would be a case of first come first served for the rest of the population, with a Martian alternative. The Bank Manager was certain that the name of Noah would ensure a ticket on the VIP flight if Mr Noah wished to change his mind, and accept a lift out by his balloon?

'For soon you Noahs will be all alone in this world with only the animals for company,' he said. 'Will you not find that rather lonely?'

'Thank you, but we never have before,' said Mr Noah. 'It will be an interesting challenge to repopulate it in due course, when the waters have receded, with the assistance of my sons and daughters-in-law and my passengers.'

'But when the waters *have* receded, will there not be something of a problem in locating any olive trees—or indeed any trees at all—this time?' said the Bank Manager, 'such as I suggested on my last visit?'

Mr Noah had been having trouble with the consistency of the pitch on the last visit, and as usual had not heard a word the Bank Manager had said, but did not like to hurt his feelings now, so: 'Ah, *that*,' he said cheerfully, 'that will all resolve itself: after all the highest mountains will show through first, so there will be excellent drainage and things will soon dry off everywhere. Our Doves should experience no difficulty.'

'Then Bon Voyage to the Ark and all who sail with you, Mr Noah,' said the Bank Manager rather dubiously.

A Second Roll-call

Mr Noah stood at the top of the gangway with a loudhailer fashioned from a buffalo horn: 'Aardvark, Addax, Anoa, Anteater, Armadillo, Aye-aye . . .' he would call through it, or 'Baboon, Badger, Bandicoot, Bears, Bison . . .' and each species present would answer according to its wont, then proceed two by two up the gangway, where they were welcomed aboard and ticked off the list.

The animals were all most courteous and helpful to each other, the larger ones watching carefully where they put their feet to avoid treading on the very small ones, and those with antlers and tusks making sure that they did not get in the way. They found their quarters easily and settled in. The Giraffes were particularly pleased with the headroom in theirs, and the nocturnal animals were delighted to find that they had a quiet separate section aft with heavy light-excluding curtains at the windows.

But long before he was half-way through the C's Mr Noah was becoming increasingly perturbed at the number of names that went unanswered.

He knew, of course, that there were several species on the ancestral list that could be crossed out, and he had not for one minute expected a Giant Sloth or a Sabretoothed Tiger any more than the original Captain Noah had anticipated welcoming a Woolly Mammoth or a Brontosaurus aboard; nor did he believe in Unicorns or Yeti. But the silence that followed name after name today was unnerving. And he knew that it was not a question of those whose names began with the latter letters of the alphabet arriving later to avoid waiting around too long before embarkation, because he had already explained to the Wallabies why they could not enter behind the Kangaroos, however alike they looked, and he remembered seeing a pair of Yapocks playing around in the puddles with the local Otters several days before.

It was the silence of the great cats as the day wore on that particularly upset him, for he had always admired them and had looked forward to having them as shipmates. 'Cheetah, Cougar, Jaguar, Lynx, Leopard, Lion, Ocelot . . .' he had called and called at intervals through his buffalo horn in vain. Then, at last, late in the afternoon, to his 'Tiger, Tiger . . .', to his great joy he saw a stripy figure moving up slowly through the column of anmimals, who parted respectfully to let it through, and at last an old, very shabby Tiger limped into view and stood at the end of the gangway.

'Do come aboard,' said Mr Noah, relieved, but wondering why such a tottery specimen had been sent to represent his race. But the Tiger shook his head and remained at the bottom of the gangway.

'Are you waiting for your wife?' Mr Noah called, but the Tiger shook his head again and sadly sniffed the buttercups and daisies. Mr Noah hurried down.

Unexpectedly, the Tiger was able to speak, although with difficulty, as he had no teeth. He had come from Kernafuli, in Bengal, he said, and as far as he knew he was the only one left, for his wife had fallen to a sporting oil magnate's rifle on the way and was now a rug in the sportsman's yacht. If he hadn't been so undecorative himself he would probably be stretched out there beside her. And no, he had not seen any Ocelot, Lynx, Leopard or indeed any of his great cat cousins on the way—or for years for that matter. He fully realized, he went on, that he could not take up a single space in the Ark, for that would defeat the whole purpose of the Voyage, but if Mr Noah did not mind he would take his place at the very end of the queue in the hope that there might be some lone lady tiger somewhere in the world who might yet turn up to accompany him?

Sheila Burnford

The Judgement Flood

The great storm will come when Monday's a day,
    All the world of the air will outpour,
And through all its lasting we shall obey,
    We whose ears will be filled with its roar.

The freezing will come when Tuesday's a day,
    All pain to the heart and piercing fine,
Flecking from the cheeks, though pale of array,
    Blood as red as the red-pouring wine.

The wind it will blow when Wednesday's a day,
    Sweeping bare down the strath and the plain,
Sharp-showering the gusts that cut and slay,
    Thunderclaps and mountains split in twain.

The rain it will pour when Thursday's a day,
    Driving men into blind rushing flight,
Faster than leaves which scurry from the spray,
    A-shake like Mary's plant-leaves in fright.

The dark cloud will come when Friday's a day,
    The direst dread that ever was known,
Multitudes left with their reason astray,
    Grass and fish underneath the one stone.

The great sea will come when Saturday's a day,
    Full of anger, full of sorrow's pain,
As he hears the bitter words all men say,
    A red cross on each right shoulder lain.

Gaelic

After the second flood there may be many new and strange animals. Dougal Dixon has looked fifty million years ahead to see what animals may evolve after man. His new species range from

A

Land-dwelling animals that have taken to an aquatic mode of life have usually done so initially to escape land-dwelling predators. This is probably why the water ant has taken to building its huge nests on rafts in swamps and backwaters. Each nest is made of twigs and fibrous vegetable material, waterproofed by a plaster of mud. It is connected to the banks and to floating foodstores by a network of bridges and ramps. However, in their new mode of life the ants are still vulnerable to the swimming **ant-eater** which has evolved in parallel with it. The ant-eater lives solely on the water ants, and to reach them undetected it attacks the nest from below, ripping through the waterproof shell with its clawed paddles. Since below the waterline the nest is made of discrete chambers that can rapidly be made watertight in an emergency, little damage is done to the colony as a whole.

to Z

The **zarander** lives on the spare herbs and shrubs found in less dense areas of the forest floor. Its long trunk, developed from a snout similar to the trunk of the ancient elephant, enables the zarander to reach leafy branches four metres above the ground, where it can snip branches and vines from the trees by the scissor action of its upper and lower tusks. Despite its long nose the zarander has little sense of smell. Like other mammals of the forest floor, the lack of wind and general circulation among the dense trees means that scents do not travel far. Relying on its keen hearing to warn it of the approach of an enemy, it takes off into the thicker parts of the forest at the arrival of a predator, squeezing its narrow body between the tree trunks, and remaining motionless, camouflaged by its stripes and dark body colour.

Dougal Dixon

Postscript

Kliwa! Ye! O! Rainbow, O rainbow!
You who shine on high, so high,
Above the great forest,
Among the black clouds,
Dividing the black sky.

Beneath you you have overturned,
Victor in the struggle,
The thunder which growled,
Which growled so strongly in its wrath
Was it angry with us?

Among the black clouds,
Dividing the dark sky,
Like the knife which cuts a too ripe fruit,
Rainbow, rainbow!

He has taken flight,
The thunder, the man-killer,
Like the antelope before the panther,
He has taken flight,
Rainbow, rainbow!

Mighty bow of the hunter on high,
Of the hunter who chases the herd of clouds,
Like a herd of frightened elephants,
Rainbow, tell him our thanks.

Tell him: 'Do not be angry!'
Tell him: 'Do not be provoked!'
Tell him: 'Do not kill us!'
For we are very frightened,
Rainbow, tell it to him.

Gabon Pygmy

Acknowledgements

Thanks are due to the following for permission to reprint copyright material: **Zoe Bailey:** 'Ant'. Reprinted by permission of the author. **C. M. Bowra:** 'Rainbow' from *Primitive Song*. Reprinted by permission of Weidenfeld & Nicolson Ltd. **Alan Brownjohn:** extract from 'Mole' from *Brownjohn's Beasts*. Reprinted by permission of Macmillan, London and Basingstoke. **Arthur J. Bull:** 'Deinosaurs' from *Century*. Reprinted by permission of Outposts Publications. **Sheila Burnford:** from *Mr. Noah and The Second Flood* (Gollancz). Reprinted by permission of David Higham Associates Ltd. **Roy Campbell:** 'The Zebras' from *Adamastor*. Reprinted by permission of Fransisco Campbell Custodio and Ad. Donker (Pty.) Ltd. **Brian Carter:** 'The Good Place' from *Where the Dream Begins*. Reprinted by permission of the author. **Hugh Chesterman:** 'Noah and the Rabbit'. Reprinted by permission of Basil Blackwell Publisher. **John Clare:** 'Quail's Nest' and 'The Vixen', to be published in *John Clare* (New Oxford Standard Authors, 1984). Copyright Eric Robinson; 'The Yellowhammer' from *The Later Poems of John Clare* (Manchester University Press, 1964). Reproduced by permission of Curtis Brown Academic Ltd. **Ella Clark:** from 'Mt. Rainier and the Great Flood' and for 'Mount Baker and the Great Flood', from *Indian Legends of the Pacific Northwest*, © 1953 by the Regents of the University of California Press, © 1981 by Ella E. Clark. Reprinted by permission of The University of California Press. **Leonard Clark:** 'Owls' and 'Robin Redbreast' from *The Singing Time*. Reprinted by permission of Hodder & Stoughton Children's Books. **Gregory Corso:** 'The Mad Yak' from *Long Live Man*, copyright © 1962 by New Directions Publishing Corp. Reprinted by permission of New Directions Publ. **Kevin Crossley-Holland:** 'The Swan' from *The Exeter Book of Riddles* translated by Kevin Crossley-Holland, copyright © Kevin Crossley-Holland 1965, 1970, 1978. Reprinted by permission of Deborah Rogers Ltd. **Roy Daniells:** 'Noah' from *The Chequered Shade*. Reprinted by permission of the Canadian Publishers, McClelland and Stewart Ltd., Toronto. **Peter Dickinson:** from 'Noah's Flood' from *City of Gold and Other Stories from the Old Testament*. Reprinted by permission of Victor Gollancz Ltd. **Dougal Dixon:** from *After Man: A Zoology of the Future* (Granada). Reprinted by permission of Sceptre Books. **Robert Duncan:** 'Ballad of Mrs. Noah' from *The Openings of the Field*, copyright © 1960 by Robert Duncan. Reprinted by permission of New Directions Publishing Corp. **Penelope Farmer:** 'Noj and the Flood' from *Beginnings. Reprinted by permission of Chatto & Windus Ltd*. **Michael Flanders:** from *Captain Noah and His Floating Zoo*, words by Michael Flanders (1971). Reprinted by permission of Novello & Company, Music Publ. **Roy Fuller:** 'The Giraffes' from *Collected Poems*. Reprinted by permission of André Deutsch. **Carmen Bernos de Gasztold:** extract from 'The Lizard' from *The Beasts Choir*, trs. Rumer Godden. Reprinted by permission of Macmillan, London and Basingstoke. **Wilfred Gibson:** 'The Parrots' from *Collected Poems*. Reprinted by permission of Mr. Michael Gibson and Macmillan, London and Basingstoke. **Paul Groves:** 'Hummingbird'. **Seamus Heaney:** 'Cow in Calf' from *Death of a Naturalist*. Reprinted by permission of Faber & Faber Ltd. **John Heath-Stubbs:** 'The Kingfisher'; 'The Nuthatch' and 'The Turtle Dove' from *A Parliament of Birds* (Chatto). Reprinted by permission of David Higham Associates Ltd. **Phoebe Hesketh:** 'Pigeons' from *The Buttercup Children* (Hart-Davis). Reprinted by permission of the author. **Russell Hoban:** 'The Crow' from *The Pedalling Man and Other Poems*, © 1968 by Russell Hoban. Reprinted by permission of World's Work Ltd., and Grosset & Dunlap, Inc. **Ted Hughes:** 'Wolf' and 'Woodpecker' from *Under the North Star*, by Ted Hughes, illustrated by Leonard Baskin. Text copyright © 1981 by Ted Hughes. Reprinted by permission of Faber & Faber Ltd., and Viking Penguin, Inc. 'Tigress' from *Moonbells* (published by Chatto & Windus Ltd.); 'Second Glance at a Jaguar' from *Wodwo*; 'Bullfrog' and 'An Otter' from *Lupercal*. Reprinted by permission of Faber & Faber Ltd. **K. H. Jackson:** 'The Best and Worst Nail in the Ark' from *A Celtic Miscellany*. Reprinted by permission of Routledge & Kegan Paul Ltd. **Elizabeth Jennings:** 'The Ark' from *The Secret Brother* (Macmillan); 'The Deers' Request' and 'Finale for the Animals' from *After the Ark* (Oxford University Press). Reprinted by permission of David Higham Associates Ltd. **Evan Jones:** 'Noah's Song'. Reprinted by permission of the author. **Rudyard Kipling:** ''Twas When the Rain Fell Steady', part II of *Legends of Evil*. Reprinted by permission of A. P. Watt Ltd., for The National Trust. **Vachel Lindsay:** 'Yet Gentle Will the Griffin Be' from *Collected Poems*, copyright 1914 by Macmillan Publishing Co., Inc., renewed 1942 by Elizabeth C. Lindsay. Reprinted by permission of Macmillan Publishing Co., Inc. **Douglas Livingstone:** 'Vulture' from *Sjambok and Other Poems from Africa*, © Oxford University Press 1964. Reprinted by permission of Oxford University Press. **Edward Lowbury:** 'The Unicorn' from *Green Magic* (Chatto & Windus Ltd). Reprinted by permission of the author. **George MacBeth:** 'Elephant', 'Rat', 'Rain' and 'Sand' from *Noah's Journey* (Macmillan). Reprinted by permission of the author. **G. R. D. McLean:** 'The Judgement Flood', a Gaelic poem, from *Poems of the Western Highlands*, edited by G. R. D. McLean. Reprinted by permission of The Society for Promoting Christian Knowledge. **John Mbiti:** 'Snake Song'. Reprinted by permission of the author. **Edwin Morgan:** 'Hyena' from *From Glasgow to Saturn* (Carcanet Press). Reprinted by permission of the author. **Mervyn Peake:** 'Go Little Dove' and 'Disembarkation Chorus' from *Noah's Ark*, published in *Peake's Progress* (ed. M. Gilmore, Allen Lane). Reprinted by permission of Maurice Michael, Co-Editions. **Michael Richards:** 'The Gilgamesh Flood', 'Quokka and Quoll', 'Xestobium rufovillosum' and 'Xylocoris galacticus'. Reprinted by permission of the author. **Michael Rosen:** 'Numbat' and 'Zebra Finch' were specially written for this anthology, copyright © 1982 Michael Rosen; and 'The Coming of the Phoenix Bird'. Reprinted by permission of the author. **Siegfried Sassoon:** 'Noah' from *Collected Poems* (Faber 1961). 'Thrushes' from *Selected Poems* (Faber 1968). Reprinted by permission of G. T. Sassoon. **Laurence Smith:** 'Lapwings' from *Catch the Light* (edited by Michael Harrison). Reprinted by permission of the author. **Anthony Stuart:** 'Albatross, was specially written for this anthology, © 1982 Anthony Stuart. Reprinted by permission of the author. **R. S. Thomas:** extract from 'A Blackbird is Singing' from *Collected Poems*. Reprinted by permission of Granada Publishing Ltd. **Denys Thompson:** 'The Magnificent Bull', Dinka Tribe, Africa, from *Distant Voices*, edited by Denys Thompson (Heinemann). **Gael Turnbull:**

'A Lamb'. Reprinted by permission of the author. **Rex Warner:** 'Mallard' from *Poems* (Bodley Head). Reprinted by permission of the author. **Vernon Watkins:** 'The Mare'. Reprinted by permission of Mrs. Gwen Watkins. **T. H. White:** 'Ibis', 'Upupa', 'Ursus' and 'Ibex' from *The Book of Beasts* (Cape). Reprinted by permission of David Higham Associates Ltd. **Jane Yolen:** 'Dragon Night' and 'Grandpa Bear's Lullaby', copyright © 1980 by Jane Yolen, from *Dragon Night and Other Lullabies* (Methuen). Reprinted by permission of Methuen Children's Books, London, and Methuen, Inc., New York. **Andrew Young:** 'The Eagle' from *Complete Poems*. Reprinted by permission of Martin Secker & Warburg Ltd. The publishers have made every effort to trace and contact copyright holders, but in some cases without success, and apologize for any infringement of copyright.

Illustrations
Cover: Michael Emden/Young Artists

Colour Plates
P. 17 Normil/Portal Gallery, London; photograph: Camera Press. P. 18 Rosemary Fawcett/Portal Gallery, London; photograph: Camera Press. P. 35 David Cheepen/Portal Gallery, London; photograph: Camera Press. P. 36 Maurice Wilson. P. 53 Nepetkhawi and Ibis, photograph: Ancient Art and Architecture Collection. P. 54 David Murray. P. 68 Bernard Carter/Portal Gallery, London; photograph: Camera Press. P. 64 Norma Burgin. P. 89 Toby Lyon/Portal Gallery, London; photograph: Camera Press. P. 90 13th Century manuscript illumination from *Histoire ancienne jusqu'à César*. Bibliothèque Publique de Dijon; photograph: Minirel. P. 107 'The Assuaging of the Waters' by John Martin. The Paul Mellon Centre, by kind permission of The General Assembly of the Church of Scotland. P. 109 Fred Aris/Portal Gallery, London; photograph: Camera Press. P. 125 'The Future Ark' by James Marsh. P. 126 Ronald Copas/Portal Gallery, London; photograph: Camera Press. P. 135 Sarah De'Ath. P. 136 Fergus Hall/Portal Gallery, London; photograph: Camera Press.

Black and white illustrations
Peter Bailey, Jane Lydbury, Martin White, Hugh Marshall, and Hector Fernandez who drew the A–Z of beasts and birds.

Index of titles and first lines

Albatross 36
Among the taller wood with ivy hung 79
Ant 37
Ark, The 33

Back-along, the forest was a good place; 116
Ballad of Mrs Noah, The 29
Best and Worst Nail in the Ark, The 25
Black is his colour 37
Blackbird Singing, A 38
Brown and furry 41
Bullfrog 47
But O! what Monster's this that bids me battle, 67

Captain Noah and his Floating Zoo 25, 92, 103, 113
Caterpillar 41
Coming of the phoenix bird, The 99
Coo-oo, coo-oo 120
Cow in Calf 122
Crocodile, A 120
Crow, The 40

Deer's Request, The 43
Deinosaurs 96
Delicate mother Kangaroo 57
Disembarkation chorus 114
Dragon-Fly, The 42
Dragon Night 97

Eagle, The 44
Elephant comes last in his loose grey skins. In 45

Finale for the Animals 124
Flying loose and easy, where does he go 40
From the dark woods that breathe of fallen showers 87

Gilgamesh Flood, The 6
Giraffes, The 49
Go little Dove, alone, alone 109
Good Place, The 116
Grandpa Bear's Lullaby 123

140

Hard by the lilied Nile I saw 120
He hangs between his wings outspread 44
Here comes the squealing 58
Hollow Wood, The 48
Humming Bird, The 50
Hyena 50

I am waiting for you 50
I am watching them churn the last milk 85
I caught this morning morning's minion, king- 46
I love the Deinosaurs, their padded bulk 96
I think before they saw me the giraffes 49
I wandered out one rainy day 68
Ibex 52
Ibis 52
It seems she has swallowed a barrel 122
It seems wrong that out of this bird 38

Jackdaw, The 54
Judgement Flood, The 131

Kangaroo 57
Khwa! Ye! O! Rainbow, O rainbow! 137
Kingfisher, The 56

Lamb, A 121
Lapwings 58
Little flame mouths 97
Lizard, The 59
Look hard enough, and you will find, 98
Lord 59

Mad Yak, The 85
Magnificent Bull, The 39
Mallard 60
Mare, The 122
Mole 61
Mount Baker and the Great Flood 10
Mount Rainier and the Great Flood 8
Mrs Noah in the Ark 29
My bull is white like the silver fish in the river 39

Neither legs nor arms have I 73
'No land,' said Noah 34

141

Noah (Chester Miracle Play) 19, 91, 102
Noah (Roy Daniells) 31
Noah (Siegfried Sassoon) 111
Noah and the Rabbit 34
Noah's Song 105
Nobody knows just how they went 33
Noj and the Flood 11
Numbat, The 62
Nuthatch, The 62

O Albatross 36
On the banks of the Nile 99
On ragged black sails 78
One day, one day 106
Otter, An 65
Out in the sun the goldfinch flies 48
Owls 64

Parrots, The 66
Pigeons 110
Pigeon and Wren 120
Please do not confuse us two 69
Porcupine, On the 67
Postscript 137

Quail's Nest 68
Quokka and Quoll 69

Rain is the one who goes on. He is flung 94
Rat leaves a sinking ship. Wise 71
Raven 106
Robin Redbreast 70

Sand clutches the keel in his cool 115
Second Ark, A 127
Second Glance at a Jaguar 55
She grin-lifts 74
Silent is my dress when I step across the earth 72
Skinfull of bowls, he bowls them, 55
Slate-blue above, buff below 62
Snake Song, The 73
So disembark! The storm has found its ending 114
Some with cruelty came, sharp-fanged and clawed 124
Somewhere, somewhen I've seen 66
Squawking they rise from reeds into the sun 60
Swan, The 72

The animals are silent in the hold 105
The great storm will come when Monday's a day 131
The humming bird refuels 50
The Iron Wolf, the Iron Wolf 81
The mare lies down in the grass where the nest of the skylark is hidden 122
The moon? It is a griffin's egg 100
The night is long 123
Then, as the lifted land lay upwards 106
There is a bird called the IBIS . . . 52
There is a bird who by his coat 54
There is an animal called IBEX the Chamois 52
There was scurrying and scrimmage when the wild ones all escaped 116
Thrushes 74
Thrush's Nest, The 123
They gathered around and told him not to do it 31
They haunt the garden now, the pair of them 110
They stare at you 64
Tigress 74
To have to be a mole? 61
To-day I saw the dragon-fly 42
Tossed on the glittering air they soar and skim 74
Turtle Dove, The 106
'Twas when the rain fell steady 32

Underwater eyes, an eel's 65
Unicorn, The (Edward Lowbury) 98
Unicorn, The (Folk Tale) 97
Upupa 76
Ursus 77

Vixen, The 79
Vulture 78

We are the disappearers 43
When Noah left the Ark, the animals 56
When old Noah stared across the floods 111
When shall I see the white-thorn leaves again 84
When the animals were let out of the Ark after the flood 116
Windhover, The 46
With their lithe long strong legs 47
Within a thick and spreading hawthorn bush 123
Wolf 81
Woodpecker is rubber-necked 80

Xestobium nifovillosum 83
Xylocoris galactinus 82

Yellowhammer, The 84
Yes, I saw a lamb where they've built a new housing 121
Yet gentle will the griffin be 100
You are a strange bird 70

Zebra Finch 86
Zebras, The 87